TRAVELLERS

PERU

By
JANE EGGINTON

Written by Jane Egginton, updated by Robin Gauldie
Original photography by Iain MacIntyre

Published by Thomas Cook Publishing
A division of Thomas Cook Tour Operations Limited.
Company registration no. 3772199 England
The Thomas Cook Business Park, Unit 9, Coningsby Road,
Peterborough PE3 8SB, United Kingdom
E-mail: books@thomascook.com, Tel: + 44 (0) 1733 416477
www.thomascookpublishing.com

Produced by Cambridge Publishing Management Limited
Burr Elm Court, Main Street, Caldecote CB23 7NU

ISBN: 978-1-84848-144-2

First edition © 2007 Thomas Cook Publishing
This second edition © 2009
Text © Thomas Cook Publishing
Maps © Thomas Cook Publishing/PCGraphics (UK) Limited

Series Editor: Maisie Fitzpatrick
Project Editor: Lucy Armstrong
Production/DTP: Steven Collins

Printed and bound in Italy by Printer Trento

Cover photography: Front L-R: © Kavita Favelle/Alamy; © Design Pics Inc./
Alamy; © Orient/4CR
Back: © Bruno Cossa/4CR

Contents

Introduction

The cradle of the Inca Empire is, in many ways, a living museum. Peru's main sights are not tucked away in dusty collections, but laid out for all to see across its scenic landscapes. Indeed, in many cases, they are the landscapes. The country is no longer the 'deepest, darkest Peru' of Paddington Bear fame. Although undeniably exotic, its highlights are on well-travelled routes and, as one of the most popular destinations in South America, Peru is used to welcoming international visitors.

Machu Picchu is not just a highlight of Peru, but of the world. A dizzying architectural achievement, the legendary lost city is perched high on an Andean mountain. It is reached on foot by one of the most famous expeditions in the world – a five-day trek along the Machu Picchu trail, or by train on the evocative Orient Express. This luxurious train service also takes travellers through the mountains from Cusco down to the shores of Lake Titicaca, where visitors can take a scenic boat trip among floating islands of reeds. Other wonderful journeys come in the form of rainforest trails through the dense Amazon jungle and a flight over the desert for the best view of the giant, enigmatic figures etched in the sand by the ancient Nazca people.

In Lima, the capital, there are treasure troves, such as the Gold Museum with its glittering exhibits, and colonial history can be seen in the churches and cathedrals where the local population still worship. The city of Cusco – whose name means 'belly button of the world' – is the archaeological centre of the country. Pre-Columbian monuments sit side by side with its colonial cathedral and convent, and the surrounding Sacred Valley is dotted with important ruins and lovely traditional villages. Arequipa is Peru's 'White City', its fine 18th-century buildings made of the local gleaming stone, while Chán Chán is one of the largest adobe (hard, dried mud) cities in the world, capital of a civilisation that predates even the Incas.

Peru's natural wonders extend to pristine snow-covered mountains that the adventurous can climb, and the little-known Colca Canyon. This gorge is actually twice as deep as the Grand Canyon and a popular place to see the condor – one of the largest flying birds in the world. There are birds in the jungle too, typically brightly coloured like the parrot and the toucan, as well as playful monkeys and fierce caimans.

Steep terracing forms deep scars in the green hills where local people have left their mark over the centuries and where they continue to farm.

Peruvian culture comes alive in its colourful festivals and through the rich textiles and handicrafts sold on almost every street corner. Music and dance are at the heart of the national consciousness and express not just the rich history, but also the daily life of the people.

In Peru, a simple walk down the street or in the countryside can take you straight to the heart of the country and its very essence.

A condor flies over the Mirador

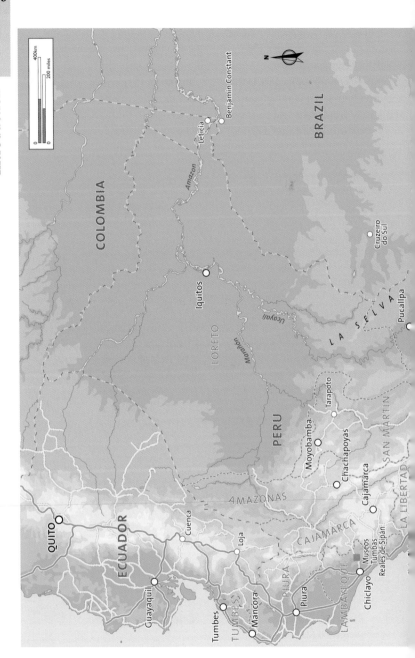

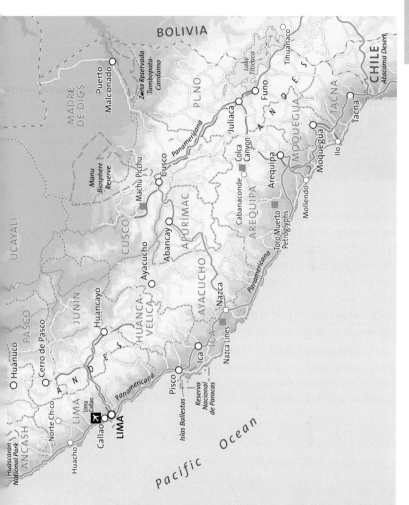

City
Large Town
Small Town
POI
Motorway
Main Road
Minor Road
Airport
Railway

The land

The third-largest country in South America is five times the size of Great Britain and counts five countries as its neighbours. All of Peru's land lies within the tropics, with its northernmost point falling just below the equator. The Spanish divided Peru into three regions – the tropical jungle in the east, the dusty desert plains in the west and the chilly mountains in the high Andes – a variety of landscapes as diverse as a continent.

Despite a long Pacific coastline that stretches from Ecuador down to Chile, Peru has few dazzling beaches. Many have dark brown gritty sand and often they are backed by main roads. Perhaps the best beaches are at Trujillo in the north and at Mancora, where the waves that pound the shore make for a surfers' playground. South of Lima, the sea has sculpted the land into the curve of the Paracas Peninsula, and caused the land to break off to form the Ballestas Islands, an area rich in marine and bird life. Much of this land, and the ocean around it, is now the Paracas National Reserve.

The Peruvian section of the Pan-American Highway, the Panamericana, stretches the whole length of the country, connecting all the major coastal settlements. Here, the Andes tumble dramatically downwards towards the sea, interrupted only by a thin strip of land that is mostly

The dramatic desert coastline of the Ica region, south of Lima

The Amazon river and jungle

desert. In some places, there are sweeping, scenic dunes, but in others a barren moonscape with little visual relief. Just over the border with Chile, the Atacama Desert is the driest place on the planet.

The central highland area is dominated by the pronounced spine of the Andes – Peru's breadbasket and home to the vast majority of its population. The roads here are often tortuous and in terrible condition, but the views are spectacular. The snow-covered mountains of the Andes are some of the highest peaks in the world. Within Huascarán National Park are Nevada Huascarán (6,768m/22,206ft) and 40 other challenging climbs over 6,000m (19,700ft), in a breathtaking landscape that includes 200 alpine lakes, hundreds of glaciers and numerous pre-Columbian ruins.

On its eastern side, the vast mountain range of the Andes flattens out to create gentle foothills and an area known as La Selva. Further east is the vast, relatively untouched rainforest region making up more than half of the country. Here is the Amazon basin where the mighty river has its source, and where two other big rivers, the Marañón and the Ucayali, collide. More than 20 national parks protect this important region that has, nevertheless, suffered from deforestation. Manu Biosphere Reserve is one of the biggest and best protected, with an incredible variety of habitats, such as tropical lowland forest, mountain forest and grasslands. Tambopata-Candamo Reserve Zone is similar and, although less well known, is in fact easier to visit.

Peru's far southeastern corner is home to two of the country's most scenic sights: Lake Titicaca, the highest navigable lake in the world, and the Colca Canyon, one of the deepest on the planet.

History

20,000–10,000 BC	Earliest nomads, probably from Asia, arrive in Peru.	**1000**	The appearance of the Chimú culture.
5000–3000 BC	Inhabitants learn how to plant crops. Cotton is cultivated thousands of years before the technique is known to Europeans.	**1150**	The Chimú begin construction of Chán Chán, which becomes home to 50,000 people.
3000–1800 BC	The first complex society in the Americas develops in the bleak Norte Chico region of Peru.	**1200**	Chimú and Chancay cultures established; Manco Cápac becomes the first Inca (emperor) and founds the Inca Empire.
900–200 BC	Chavín culture comes to dominate northern Peru. A grand monumental centre is established at Chavín de Huántar, and their intricate art is seen far and wide in metallurgy, textiles and ceramics. At the same time, Paracas culture takes root in the south of Peru.	**1350**	Inca Roca (the sixth Inca) establishes the Cusco dynasty.

300 BC–AD 700 Nazca culture grows in southern Peru.

AD 200 Northern Peru under the grip of the Moche Dynasty.

300 The burial of the Lord of Sipán.

375–500 Rise of the Wari-Tiahuanaco Empire.

Celebrating the Inca Winter Solstice

1400	Tschudi Palace at Chán Chán built.
1438–71	Inca Pachacútec builds Sacsayhuamán and Machu Picchu.
1460 onwards	The Inca Empire expands, reaching the southern desert coast.
1465	Inca domination of the territory from the northern Andes to Ecuador.
1527	Epidemic of smallpox fells the Inca Huayna Cápac. The kingdom is split into two and civil war breaks out.
1530	Francisco Pizarro's third expedition arrives in Tumbes from Panama.
1532	Atahualpa, son of Huayna Cápac, takes control of the Inca Empire but is captured by Francisco Pizarro.
1533	The Spanish kill Atahualpa and raze Cusco.
1535	Francisco Pizarro establishes Lima and makes it the capital of the Viceroyalty of Peru.
1541	Francisco Pizarro is killed in Lima.
1572	Tupac Amaru, the last Inca emperor, is captured and executed by the Spanish, marking the end of the Inca empire.
1780	An Indian noble, Tupac Amaru II, leads a doomed uprising against the Spanish.
1821	General José de San Martín captures Lima and then proclaims that Peru is independent.
1824	Peruvian forces finally defeat the remnants of the Spanish army.
1849–74	Tens of thousands of Chinese immigrants are employed as cheap labour to service the Amazonian rubber boom.
1879–83	Chile defeats both Peru and Bolivia in the War of the Pacific.
1924	From exile in Mexico, Victor Raúl Haya de la Torre sets up the nationalist American Popular Revolutionary Alliance (APRA).

1941	Peru and Ecuador clash over the northern Amazon.
1945	Civilian government led by APRA takes power after free elections.
1948	A coup d'état installs a military government led by General Manuel Odría.
1963	Peru returns to civilian rule; Fernando Belaúnde Terry becomes the president.
1968	The civilian government is ousted in a coup led by left-wing General Juan Velasco Alvarado, who undertakes land reform and nationalisation of industry and banks.
1975	General Morales Bermúdez takes power in yet another coup.
1980	The 'Shining Path' Communist Party turns from largely peaceful protest to all-out war. Another group, Tupac Amaru (MRTA), launches its own armed struggle.
1981	Peru fights Ecuador in a border dispute over the Cordillera del Cóndor.
1982	The army gets tough on the Shining Path, and atrocities against civilians take place.
1985–90	Alan García (APRA) wins power. Country falls into chaos as hyperinflation cripples the economy. The Shining Path expands its campaign to cities and becomes even more ruthless.
1990	Alberto Fujimori, the son of Japanese immigrants, is elected president and begins a programme of privatisation and austerity, combined with a crackdown on drugs terror and guerrilla fighters.
1992	Former Shining Path leader Abimael Guzmán is arrested and sentenced to life in prison by a military court.
1993	Alberto Fujimori changes the constitution so he can stand again for president.
1995	Alberto Fujimori is re-elected. More border clashes with Ecuador.
1997	El Niño causes the worst storm of the century and

brings a harsh drought to large parts of Peru.

1999   Ecuador and Peru agree to settle their differences over the Amazon.

2000   Alberto Fujimori is elected for a third time but is embroiled in charges of fraud and corruption. He resigns by fax from Japan.

2001   Alejandro Toledo becomes first president of native Indian origin and makes an inaugural visit to Machu Picchu. Arequipa is struck by a massive earthquake.

The President's palace in Lima's Plaza de Armas

2002   The Shining Path bombs the US embassy in Lima.

2003   Workers go on strike, and a state of emergency is declared.

2005   Congress finds President Toledo guilty of electoral fraud, but votes not to impeach him.

2006   Alan García is elected president on a social improvement programme, despite a calamitous first term in office between 1985 and 1990. Former Shining Path leader Abimael Guzmán is retried by a civilian court and receives a new life sentence.

2007   At least 600 people are killed by an earthquake in the Pisco and Ica regions.

2009   The trial of former president Alberto Fujimori for human rights violations concludes.

2011   Presidential and congressional elections are due.

Ancient civilisations

At a time when the coastal dwellers of Peru were simple hunter-gatherers, the region of Norte Chico, spread over three bleak valleys in the interior, housed a complex civilisation that was unearthed only in 2004. The discovery suggests that as early as 3000 BC the people in this region built complex irrigation systems, competed to build grand pyramids, and set up trade with the coastal fishermen. This would indicate an organised society, and qualifies Norte Chico as the earliest civilisation in the whole of the Americas.

Becoming unequal

There is evidence too that the pre-ceramic Norte Chico influenced the Chavín culture that flourished in the

Tschudi Palace at Chán Chán

2nd century BC. The intricate and detailed Chavín style can be seen in their pottery and metalwork, and in the monumental centre they constructed at Chavín de Huántar, 250km (155 miles) north of Lima. Today, some of the Chavín reliefs from this archaeological site are on display in the Museo de la Nación in Lima (*see p32*). Chavín de Huántar has been declared a UNESCO World Heritage Site, although it is in need of much work if it is to fulfil its potential as 'the next Machu Picchu'.

The most interesting point about Norte Chico and the Chavín is that they encapsulate a key point in human existence when we stopped being 'equal'. States were formed, with different individuals and groups wielding different amounts of power and prestige, usually under a strong hereditary leadership.

Road to the Incas

Of course, when we think of organised pre-Columbian societies, the Incas (*see p66*) come to mind, but, while their empire covered great swathes of South America, it was short-lived. Before their domination, a succession of geographically and culturally diverse societies coexisted. For example, the Paracas peoples dominated the south around the time that the Chavín ruled the north. The Paracas excelled in the weaving of fine, ornate burial clothes, which were discovered in a huge necropolis in 1950.

The Chavín were succeeded by the militaristic Moche dynasty (*see p116*) that left behind spectacular tombs at Sipán and wonderful erotic ceramics. In the south, the Paracas were succeeded by the Nazca, who excelled at pottery but also produced some of the most mind-boggling art ever seen – gigantic geometric forms and animals etched into the ground over hundreds of square kilometres of desert, and really visible only from the sky (the Nazca Lines).

South again from Nazca territory is Lake Titicaca, which Peru shares with Bolivia. On the southern shore of the lake, Tiahuanaco was a major civilisation from AD 700, making extensive use of stone for architecture, sculpture and ceremonial objects. From AD 1000, northern Peru was dominated by the Chimú, who built the huge adobe city of Chán Chán (*see p114*), where 100,000 people lived.

But in 1200, as legend has it, Manco Cápac (the first Inca – emperor) left Lake Titicaca at the

The Sun God, father of the first Inca

request of the Sun God to found a new civilisation in the highlands. The governing 'Sapa Incas' of this society went on to build Cusco and Machu Picchu. They dominated the land from the northern Andes into Ecuador, and ruled large parts of what are now Peru, Bolivia, Argentina and Chile. They built paved roads to sustain their far-flung empire, so that troops and supplies could be transported where they were needed. Their laws were strict, and their society was fiercely hierarchical, but their subjects were given work, food and a unifying purpose. To defend the empire, they built imposing mountain-top fortresses, and created a professional army of some 40,000 men. And yet this empire was defeated at the height of its powers by a Spanish conqueror whose troops numbered less than 200 (*see p11*).

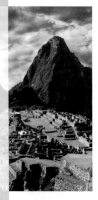

Politics

In Peru, Independence Day is celebrated on 28 July. This was the day in 1821 that José de San Martín was inaugurated as the country's first president. In the next eight years, the leadership was to change hands ten times, before the country's first coup d'état overthrew former independence hero José de la Mar. Since 1990, however, things have become gradually more stable, both politically and economically.

FujiShock

The biggest scandal of recent years surrounds President Fujimori. In 2000, he became embroiled in a votes-for-cash scandal after being elected to his third term as president.

Immediately after his first election victory in 1990, Fujimori, taking over from Alan García (1985–90), initiated a programme of economic austerity aimed at tackling the country's hyperinflation. The policy became known as *FujiShock*, partly because of its harshness, and partly because it was the exact opposite of the platform he had just campaigned on. Price controls and subsidies were removed, and trade was liberalised. Within a year, inflation had fallen from a staggering 7,650 per cent to a more manageable 139 per cent.

In 1992, Fujimori launched a coup d'état against his own government, dissolving the opposition-led congress, and establishing a new one that would rubber-stamp his legislation. Fujimori quickly assumed emergency powers to deal with terrorism, leading to curfews, censorship, and arrest without charge. But, in the eyes of the people, these shock tactics bore fruit when the Shining Path's leader was arrested and sentenced by a military court to life imprisonment (*see p56*).

Man of the people

As in many South American countries, an invisible wall has kept people of indigenous and African descent away from positions of power in Peru. So, the appointment in 2001 of Alejandro

Alberto Fujimori, president from 1990 to 2001

Toledo as the county's first indigenous *campesino* (farm worker) president was a milestone. He was one of 16 brothers and sisters, six of whom died when he was young, and he came to power on a wave of goodwill, notwithstanding accusations that he had previously taken cocaine, cavorted with prostitutes, and abandoned his illegitimate child.

San Isidro business district in Lima

Despite continued press criticism during the early years of his presidency, Toledo allowed democracy and the press to flourish. He presided over an economic regeneration, with consistently low inflation, and year-on-year economic growth of 5 per cent, aided by a new trade agreement with the US. He reduced the number of people living below the poverty line by 6 per cent overall during his term – though by his own admission, with 48 per cent of Peruvians still in poverty, this was not enough.

Back to the future
Alan García made a comeback to win the presidential elections of 2006, but his APRA party won only 36 seats in the congressional elections held the same year, against 45 seats that went to its main rival, Unión por el Perú. From the 24 parties contesting the elections, the right-wing Unidad Nacional won 17 seats, the centre-right Alianza por el Futuro won 13, the centrist Frente del Centro won five and the fringe parties Perú Posible and Restauración Nacional each won two seats. Without a majority in Congress, Alan García has therefore had to tread a cautious political path. Nevertheless, his government claimed to have reduced Peru's poverty index by eight points in its first two years and was optimistic that measures including closer trade links with the European Union would help tackle Peru's economic problems.

Final disgrace for Fujimori
In September 2007 the disgraced Alberto Fujimori was extradited from Chile to face trial in Peru for alleged human rights offences during his time in power. The trial dragged on for more than a year, well into 2009.

Looking ahead
Alan García and the Apristas face presidential and congressional elections in 2011. Peru's political future will depend not only on whether the current administration can manage the country's economy through a global recession, but also on whether a more unified opposition can emerge with a convincing set of alternative policies to put before Peru's people.

Culture

Peruvian culture is rich, and it is also deeply rooted in its history. Throughout the country, music, dance, art, architecture and literature are mestizo *– a 'mix' of influences from its sophisticated pre-Columbian societies, the Spanish invaders, African slaves and contemporary visionaries. This can be seen not only in Peru's museums and churches, but also in its vibrant festivals (see p22) and even in its handicraft shops. Peru's culture is renowned far beyond its borders, and is one of the biggest attractions for visitors.*

Art and architecture

The pre-Inca cultures created intricate pieces of early art in the form of decorative pottery, jewellery and textiles that were some of the most impressive in the world at that time. The Incas went on to achieve spectacular feats in architecture – the best example is the monumental Machu Picchu. When the Spanish arrived in the early 16th century, it resulted in *mestizo* architecture – created by the collision between the Hispanic and Amerindian societies and best seen in the churches around Puno and Arequipa.

In the same way, the Spanish colonists combined with the Indians to create a Creole form of art – one of the most important in the country. The Cusco School was famous throughout the colonial period for its religious expressions from a Native American perspective. In the 21st century, art in Peru is both modern, drawing on the tradition of fine as well as abstract art, and indigenous, continuing to make use of natural materials and rooted in experience.

Music

The latest archaeological discoveries show that Peru's musical traditions date

Ornate door-knocker at Lima Cathedral

Religious art above a doorway in Arequipa's Convento de Santa Catalina

back 10,000 years. Unlike its art, Peruvian music is essentially folk, with regional variations. Like the country's artists, the musicians made use of their local materials, so that trumpets (*pututos*) were made from sea conches, willowy cane was used to create wind instruments, and a kind of mandolin known as a *charango* was crafted from the shell of armadillos. Today, most instruments are fashioned from wood, so that the flute-like *quena*, once made of llama bone, is now made of bamboo.

The pan pipes most people associate with Peru produce a range of pitches. Percussion – such as the tambar and bombo drum – is important too, and, when the Spanish came, they brought string instruments with them, a form of which is still heard today. In the 18th century, the introduction of African slaves led to a kind of Creole music. Forbidden from beating actual drums, the slaves beat packing cases that evolved into the wooden box known as the *cajón* – a percussive form that only became popular with the general population in the 20th century.

True to the spirit of any living art form, the music in Peru continues to evolve. The latest instruments from the West, such as synths and electric guitars, have been embraced, and new genres created such as *chicha*, an urban brew of traditional and rock music. Music in Peru is not restricted to theatres or stages or even festivals. It is heard on every street corner, in homes, in cantinas and on CD systems here and around the world.

Dance

La Marinera is the most typical dance of Peru, and is performed throughout the country, but its capital is certainly the northern city of Trujillo. There are obvious regional variations – in Lima the dance is more elegant, and in the north it tends to be imitative of horse-riding. With its roots firmly in the African and indigenous traditions, La Marinera is nonetheless evocative of the Spanish flamenco. Dancers whirl passionately to a clapping rhythmic soundtrack of guitars and *cajon* drums. The dominating man wears a straw hat, while the barefoot female partner is flirtatious in a layered skirt.

The unusual Scissors dance also displays distinct Spanish elements – such as the musical metal sheets (forming a kind of scissor) that echo the sound of castanets. This is dance as deep ritual, as religious offering. It dates back to the time when the Andean religion was all but destroyed by the Christian invaders. When the temples and then the homes in which it was practised were smashed, the only hiding place was the body – and these dances are an expression of this. The dancers make dramatic jumps, pierce their tongues and balance harps on their heads, usually as part of a festival, feast day or cleansing ritual.

The Diablada – the Devil's Last Dance – is a demonstration of the victory of good over evil, and typical of Puno Festejo (Puno Festival) is a fast, sensual dance of rhythmical nature that is, as its name suggests, typically a celebration. The Tondero Dance represents the rooster's pursuit of the chicken. These are just some of the examples of the fascinating repertoire of traditional dance that continues in Peru today.

Literature

Before the arrival of the Spanish, Peruvian culture was inextricably linked with religious and ceremonial expressions. The first work of literature to come from Peru was *Comentarios Reales de los Incas* (*Royal Commentaries of the Incas*), a prose narrative written in 1609 by Garcilaso de la Vega, the *mestizo* offspring of a Spanish conquistador and an Inca princess.

Ricardo Palma (1833–1919) created a unique literary genre known as *tradición*, in which history was practically indistinguishable from fiction. Although his works cannot be relied upon for their factual accuracy, they form an undeniably fascinating and important chronicle of the spirit of his age. The revolutionary Manuel González Prada was another writer very much of his time, using both prose and poetry to denounce the colonialists in the late 19th century. When Clorinda Matto de Turner (1852–1909) penned *Aves sin Nido* (*Birds without a Nest*) in 1889, she was one of the first white Peruvian authors to write about indigenous themes.

However, in the end she was deemed so controversial that she was forced to flee the country.

The 20th century spawned a number of significant Peruvian writers, the most celebrated of whom is Mario Vargas Llosa. He temporarily gave up his luminary writing career to run unsuccessfully for president, and then went on in 1993 to write *El Pez en el Agua* (*A Fish in the Water*) about his experience. In this country where a poet can stand for president, culture is more than an abstract concept – it is intrinsically linked with the nation's past, present and future.

Dancing the Marinera in Trujillo

Festivals and events

Many Peruvian festivals are distinctly religious – honouring Christ, the Virgin Mary or the patron saints – and can be quite solemn. Some are political, even patriotic. Others are part of the farming calendar and one of the only chances for poor Peruvians to escape grim reality. Almost all are colourful and may involve parades, traditional costumes and dance, and fireworks.

Movable feasts

Some of Peru's festivities are movable feasts, changing dates from year to year, such as Carnival and Easter. As long as you plan carefully (hotels may be hard to come by and public transport suspended or overcrowded), experiencing one of Peru's unique festivities could well be the highlight of a holiday here.

January

Entrega de Varas, *Cusco region.* Power is handed over to new leaders (*varayocs*) symbolised by the giving of a *vara*, or wooden sceptre, in a ceremony dating back to the Incas. 1 January.

February

La Virgen de la Candelaria, *Puno.* One of Peru's most colourful festivals, involving a procession of dancers in elaborate costumes and masks, and a statue of the patron saint of the city who has assimilated characteristics of the earth goddess, Pachamama. It ends on the following Sunday with yet more dancing. 2 February.

February/March

Carnival. The most traditional celebrations are in *Cajamarca* and *Puno*. Water fights, in which tourists are targeted, are common.

March/April

Semana Santa (Holy Week). Maundy Thursday afternoon and Good Friday are public holidays. Religious processions take place throughout Peru, but are particularly impressive in *Ayacucho* and *Cusco*.

June

Corpus Christi. Religious processions, particularly in *Cusco*.
Inti Raymi. A spectacular traditional Inca ceremony, in which the sun is worshipped during the winter solstice with food, dancing and singing, and a big pageant at *Sacsayhuamán*. 24 June.

July

La Virgen del Carmen, *Paucartambo, Pisac and Pucara.* Procession with the Virgin and dancers. 16–18 July.

Independence Day. This celebrates the day in 1821 when liberator José de San Martín declared independence from the Spanish Empire. There is a speech by the president and a parade, and the next day is a holiday. A particularly busy time for travel, so book accommodation and transport in advance. 28–29 July.

August

Pachamama. Offerings to Mother Earth to mark the Andean New Year. 1 August.

September

International Spring Festival, particularly in *Trujillo.* Dancing and parades. Last week of September.

October

El Señor de los Milagros (The Lord of Miracles), *Lima.* Enormous religious procession honouring an image of a Black Christ, with devotees wearing purple. 18 October.

November

Dia de los Muertos (Day of the Dead). Food, drink and flowers are offered at family graves as part of a mostly happy celebration to remember the dead. 1 November.

Semana de Puno (Puno Week). Costumed dancers celebrate the emergence of the first Inca from Lake Titicaca, with Puno Day on the 5th as the highlight. 1–7 November.

December

Fiesta de la Purísma Concepción (Festival of the Immaculate Conception). 8 December.

The annual costumed re-creation of Inti Raymi in Cusco

Highlights

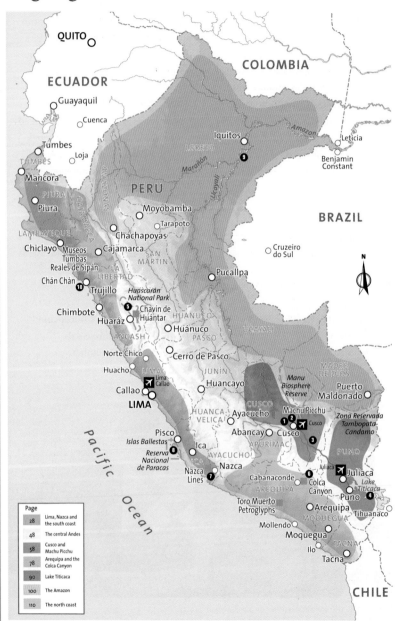

QUITO

ECUADOR

COLOMBIA

Guayaquil

Cuenca

Iquitos

Leticia

Benjamin
Constant

Tumbes

Loja

TUMBES

LORETO

Amazon

Mancora

Marañón

PERU

PIURA

Piura

AMAZONAS

Moyobamba

BRAZIL

Tarapoto

Chachapoyas

LAMBAYEQUE

Chiclayo

Museos
Tumbas
Reales de Sipán

Cajamarca

CAJAMARCA

SAN
MARTIN

Cruzeiro
do Sul

Ucayali

Chán Chán

LA
LIBERTAD

Pucallpa

Chimbote

Trujillo

Huáscarán
National Park

Chavín de
Huántar

HUÁNUCO

UCAYALI

Huaráz

ANCASH

Huánuco

PASCO

Norte Chico

Cerro de Pasco

MADRE
DE DIOS

Huacho

JUNÍN

Manu
Biosphere
Reserve

Puerto
Maldonado

LIMA
Callao

Lima
Callao

LIMA

Huancayo

CUSCO

Machu Picchu

Cusco

Zona Reservada
Tambopata-
Candamo

HUANCA-
VELICA

Ayacucho

PUNO

Pisco

Islas Ballestas

Abancay

APURIMAC

Cusco

Reserva
Nacional
de Paracas

Ica

ICA

Nazca
Lines

AYACUCHO

Nazca

Juliaca

Cabanaconde

Colca
Canyon

Juliaca

Lake
Titicaca

AREQUIPA

Toro Muerto
Petroglyphs

Puno

Arequipa

Tihuanaco

MOQUEGUA

Mollendo

Pacific Ocean

Moquegua

TACNA

Ilo

Tacna

CHILE

N

Page	
28	Lima, Nazca and the south coast
48	The central Andes
58	Cusco and Machu Picchu
78	Arequipa and the Colca Canyon
90	Lake Titicaca
100	The Amazon
110	The north coast

1 The Inca Trail Hike to Machu Picchu on one of the most spectacular walks in the world (*see p70*).

2 The Sacred Valley Explore unspoiled villages studded with Inca remains around Cusco, the 'belly button' of the world (*see p64*).

3 Railway adventure Ride the train from Cusco up to Machu Picchu or down to Puno (*see pp68 and 76*).

4 Lake Titicaca Take a ride on a boat made of reeds to tiny islands with unique communities (*see p96*).

5 Huascarán National Park Trek through this breathtaking region of snow-covered peaks and crystal-clear lakes and rivers (*see p50*).

6 Colca Canyon Make the spectacular hike down one of the biggest canyons in the world (*see p88*).

7 The Nazca Lines Fly over extraordinary, other-worldly giant sketches in the ground (*see p40*).

8 Paracas National Reserve Hike through this coastal area rich in bird and marine life (*see p43*).

9 Amazon Cruise Sail down pristine rivers deep in this magical wilderness (*see p104*).

10 Chán Chán Marvel at the little-known pre-Columbian city, the largest in the Americas (*see p114*).

Sunrise over Lake Titicaca

Suggested itineraries

Long weekend

Visitors with only a long weekend in Peru should concentrate on Cusco, the 'archaeological capital of the Americas'. International flights land at Lima, which is only an hour's plane ride to Cusco and nearby Machu Picchu, one of the unofficial wonders of the world. Allow enough time to acclimatise to the high altitude by spending a day wandering around the city with its museums and markets (*see p62*). Take another day to travel to Machu Picchu by train and another to explore the scenic delights of the Sacred Valley.

One week

In a one-week trip it is possible to walk the four- or five-day Inca Trail, with still a couple of days to spare to take in the sights of Cusco on foot (*see p62*). Alternatively, spend seven days indulging your favourite pastime, whether it's shopping in Indian markets (the ones at Cusco, nearby Pisac, Lima and Puno are all excellent), watching wildlife (the Colca Canyon and the Amazon have some special opportunities, while the Paracas National Reserve offers some of the best bird-spotting in the country) or adventure tourism (rafting the rapids near Cusco, scaling the peaks of the Andes and perhaps mountain biking in either region).

Two weeks

Two weeks allows you to see something of Lima, the 'City of Kings', on arrival, visiting all the main sights in a day, before taking a morning flight to Cusco. After a day or two acclimatising here and visiting the city's many historic sights by foot (*see p62*), take the spectacular train to Machu Picchu, and then another scenic train trip down to Puno. A boat trip on Lake Titicaca, the highest navigable lake in the world, involves a privileged encounter with the Uros island people. Finish off with a hike down the Colca Canyon, which is twice as deep as the Grand Canyon. You can avoid the day-long and very bumpy bus ride from Puno by taking a flight from nearby Juliaca to Arequipa, and a tour to the canyon from there.

Longer visits

A trip of four weeks easily allows visitors to see all of Peru's highlights, including those mentioned on the two-week itinerary. It makes sense to hire a car if travelling along the coast, as the paved Pan-American Highway follows it for the entire length. Consider hiring a car in Arequipa and driving west for a flight over the mysterious Nazca Lines. Make your way north, taking in the wine- and brandy-producing region of Ica. Stop off at the Paracas National Reserve for some sea lion spotting and a boat ride to the bird-filled Ballestas Islands.

Continue up the coast, through Lima, and on to the peaceful seaside town of Huanchaco, with its traditional fishing boats. Just a few kilometres away is Chán Chán, the largest adobe city ever built.

You could, conceivably, tack on a trip to the Amazon at the end of all this, but a visit to this impenetrable jungle can easily take a month in itself.

The Amazon Basin covers nearly half of Peru, but it is not easy to get to. The only practical access is by air, and travel within it requires a boat and experienced crew on an organised tour. Take one of the daily flights to Puerto Maldonaldo from Lima or Cusco, and visit the Tambopata Nature Reserve, teeming with exotic creatures.

Suggested itineraries

The sun rises over Machu Picchu

Lima, Nazca and the south coast

Francisco Pizarro hand-picked Lima as the headquarters of the Spanish conquistadors in 1535 for its position on the banks of the Rímac River. The Inca capital of inland Cusco was useless to the colonists as they needed a coastal centre – not least to export their Peruvian loot. Pizarro christened Lima the 'City of Kings', and it retained this prestige well into the 19th century.

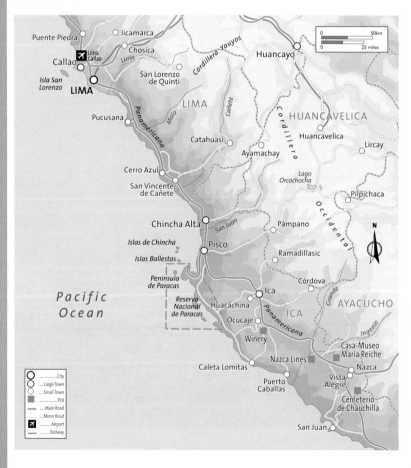

The capital has had more than its fair share of calamity. Lima is dogged by earthquakes, including one in 1746 that flattened all but a handful of buildings. Since the latter part of the 20th century, Lima has been the victim of political instability, terrorism and increasing poverty.

The chance of employment has swollen Lima's population to eight million – a third of the country – but half the city's people live in shanty towns, many barely scraping a living as *ambulantes* (street vendors).

The exquisite façade of Lima's Iglesia de la Merced

However, the city is, like its inhabitants, the Limeños, a wonderful mix of old and new, with influences from many nations. Try to avoid visiting between May and November, when a *garua*, a grey sea mist known almost affectionately as the 'belly of the donkey', shrouds the skies.

The area south of Lima is easily explored on a trip of three or four days, either by car, by bus, or partly by plane. Visit an island of birds at Ballestas and the national park at nearby Paracas. Call in at Pisco, where the key ingredient of the national drink, the Pisco Sour, is produced. End with a flight over the unforgettable Nazca Lines, where enormous figures traced in the desert by the ancient Nazca people remain an enigma to experts.

LIMA'S HISTORIC CENTRE

Old Lima is by no means the best-preserved colonial capital in South America, but it is steeped in history and has some worthwhile sights, spacious plazas and lovely carved balconies from the 18th century. The 56 blocks that make up the centre are known as *el damero de Pizarro* (Pizarro's chessboard), after the Spanish founder who laid it out on a grid. Lima's historic centre is now a UNESCO World Heritage Site – buildings are being restored, museums constructed and gardens created, resulting in a vibrant mix of old and new.

La Catedral

The cathedral, consecrated in 1625, was severely damaged by an earthquake in 1687. It was rebuilt after another earthquake in 1746 almost completely destroyed it. The interior is relatively understated, but highlights include the remains of the cathedral's founder, Francisco Pizarro, lying in a glass coffin in the tiny mosaic chapel.
East side of the Plaza de Armas.
Tel: (01) 427 9647.

Lima, Nazca and the south coast

Lima's Plaza de Armas with the Cathedral (left) and City Hall (right)

Open: 10am–1pm & 3–6pm.
Admission charge (includes entrance to
the Religious Art Museum inside).

Iglesia y Convento de San Francisco (consecrated 1673)

This spectacular yellow-and-white Baroque building was one of the few to withstand the earthquakes of 1687 and 1746. Used as a cemetery until 1810, its catacombs contain over 70,000 skeletons, some still in large wells where they were left to decompose until space could be found for them elsewhere. The church library is home to important works by Rubens and Van Dyck.

Corner of Lampa and Ancash. Open:
9.30am–5pm. Admission charge
(includes English tour).

Iglesia y Convento de Santo Domingo (completed 1599)

This church is important historically because it was built on land granted by Francisco Pizarro, and contains the tombs of Santa Rosa de Lima and of San Martín de Porras (the Americas' first black saint).

Corner of Conde de Superunda and
Camana streets. Tel: (01) 427 6793.
Church open: Mon–Sat 9am–1pm &
5–7.30pm. Convent open: Mon–Sat
9am–1pm & 3–6pm. Admission charge.

Palacio de Gobierno (rebuilt 1937)

The Government Palace is the official residence of the president, always heavily guarded, and where the changing of the guard takes place every day at noon. You should get there by 11.45am so you don't miss the colourfully dressed guardsmen goose-stepping to the national anthem, 'Somos libres', borrowed by Simon and Garfunkel for their hit 'If I Could'. It is possible to book a tour by presenting your passport at the Jefatura de Turismo at the entrance one day in advance. This will allow you to see the Dining Room and the Salón Dorado (Gold Room), which was inspired by the Hall of Mirrors in the Palace of Versailles.

North side of Plaza de Armas. Free admission.

Palacio de Torre Tagle (completed 1735)

This mansion, built by a *marqués* (marquess) who worked as treasurer for the Spanish Fleet, now houses the Ministry of Foreign Relations, swarming with security. The best example of colonial architecture in Lima, the palace fuses Spanish and Creole architectural styles, and is noted for its exquisite carved balconies and Baroque stone doorway. Visitors can only see the building from the outside and from the inner courtyard.

Ucayali 363. Courtyard open: Mon–Fri 9am–5pm. Free admission.

Lima, Nazca and the south coast

A well where bodies were stored, beneath Iglesia y Convento de San Francisco

MUSEUM CITY

Lima is home to some of the country's most impressive museums, which give visitors a good introduction to the sights in the rest of Peru. The rich collections not only are illuminating in terms of Peru's complex past, but are often exquisite objects of beauty in their own right contained in buildings with their own fascinating history. It is unlikely that you will have time to see them all, so pick two or three that match your interests.

Museo Arqueológico Rafael Larco Herrera

A well-organised museum illustrating 3,000 years of pre-Columbian history through a series of chronological galleries with ceramic, jewellery and other exhibits. Housed in an 18th-century mansion with lovely gardens, unusually the museum allows visitors to see the storage area with its 45,000 archaeological objects. The Sala Erotica is a draw for many.
Avenida Bolívar 1515, Pueblo Libre. Tel: (01) 461 1312. www.museolarco.org. Open: 9am–6pm. Admission charge.

Museo de Arte de Lima

Peruvian art spanning 3,000 years is represented in Lima's art museum, the country's best, which was designed by Gustave Eiffel. Furniture, woodcarvings and other items are on display in addition to more traditional canvases, and there is a pleasant café.
Paseo Colón 125, Parque de la Exposición. Tel: (01) 423 4732. http://museoarte.perucultural.org.pe (Spanish only). Open: Tue–Sun 9am–7pm. Admission charge.

Museo de la Inquisición

This museum is housed in a mansion that was once used as the headquarters for the Spanish Inquisition and it is now also home to a university library. There are gruesome displays of torture implements, the original cells where victims were kept, and an incredible carved ceiling in the courtroom. Judaism and homosexuality were just two of the 'crimes' proscribed by the Inquisition, which came to an end only in 1820.
Plaza Bolívar. Jirón Junín 548. Tel: (01) 311 7801. www.congreso.gob.pe/museo.htm (Spanish only). Open: 9am–5pm. Free admission, with free guided tours in English.

Museo de la Nación

Peru's National Museum is a hulking concrete building containing several floors of ceramics from a number of Peruvian ancient cultures, and replicas of finds from archaeological sites around the country. This provides an informative overview of Peru's archaeological heritage, although English translations are sometimes lacking. There are often interesting special exhibitions.

Avenida Javier Prado Este 2465. Tel: (01) 476 9875. Open: Tue–Sun 10am–5pm. Admission charge.

Museo de Oro del Perú

The museum displays a staggering amount of pre-Columbian gold and precious metal artefacts – as many as 25,000 – from a personal collection. Don't try to see everything, and be aware that many of the pieces are in fact replicas. Upstairs, there is a small weapons museum.

Alonso de Molina 1100. Tel: (01) 345 1292. www.museoroperu. com.pe. Open: noon–7pm. Admission charge.

Museo Nacional de Arqueología, Antropología e Historia del Perú

This museum of archaeology, anthropology and history has a large pre-Hispanic collection and is housed in a beautiful colonial mansion that was home first to the country's viceroys and then to its liberators. The exhibitions concentrate on Peru's history from 2000 BC until the 18th century. Textiles, ceramics, metals and art fill the rooms, and two of the most important exhibits – the Tello Obelisk and the Raimondi Stela – are carved stone pieces dating to around 1000 BC.

Plaza Bolívar, Pueblo Libre. Tel: (01) 463 5070. http://museonacional.perucultural. org.pe (Spanish only). Open: Tue–Sun 9.30am–5.30pm. Admission charge.

The front entrance to the Museo de la Nación

Lima, Nazca and the south coast

Walk: Lima – through 500 years of history

This walk begins in the Plaza de Armas, heart of the historic centre. Linger here before setting off to explore two more pretty plazas and some important museums and churches along the way.

Allow a full day for this walk of 2.5km (1½ miles) in order to appreciate all the sights and stop for lunch.

1 Plaza de Armas

This grand square (also called Plaza Mayor) is where Francisco Pizarro founded the city in 1535. Paths lead through gardens in the centre, where

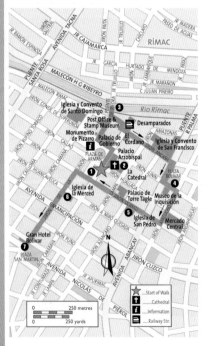

there is an elegant bronze fountain. Pause here and reflect that, although almost everything else in the city has changed, the fountain has looked like this since 1651, and it was on this spot that José de San Martín declared Peru's independence from Spain in 1821.
Step into the cathedral on the east side of the square.

2 La Catedral

At one of the side altars in the cathedral, it is possible to light a candle next to Francisco Pizarro's tomb – despite almost single-handedly wiping out the Inca race, he has been given a saint-like resting place. Nuns wander through the halls, and worshippers kneel in prayer. Rest on the cathedral steps with the locals to observe the goings-on in the square, and notice the splendid wood-carved balconies of the Archbishop's Palace that adjoins the cathedral. The Palacio de Gobierno on the north side of the plaza is worth a visit (*see p31*).

Cross the square from the cathedral and turn right, heading north along the pedestrianised street of Jirón de la Unión, passing the Monumento de Pizarro on your left, before reaching the post office and beautiful glass arcade with shops and a small museum. Continue for another half a block for a short detour to the Puente de Piedra.

3 Puente de Piedra

The historic Stone Bridge crosses the Rímac River to the now rather impoverished district of the same name where the rich once built their mansions in the 17th century.

Construction of Lima Cathedral began in 1555

Don't cross the bridge – turn back and go left along the railway track on Jirón Ancash, and stop at 100-year-old El Cordano at Ancash 202 for a jamón del norte – a typical Peruvian ham sandwich with red onion, chilli and lime. Continue one block to the Iglesia y Convento de San Francisco (see p30). Walk on for another block and a half and turn right into Avenida Abancay. Plaza Bolívar is on the left.

4 Plaza Bolívar

The central statue is of Simón Bolívar, who liberated much of South America from the Spanish. Don't miss the Museo de la Inquisición (see p32). From the southeast corner of the plaza, turn right down Jirón Ayacucho, past the Mercado Central (stop and shop if you fancy it), then turn right onto Jirón Ucayali and walk two blocks to the corner of Jirón Azángaro.

5 Iglesia de San Pedro

The plain façade of this Jesuit church constructed in 1638 belies the over-the-top Baroque interior, complete with gilded aisle.

Continuing northwest, walk half a block along Ucayali, where at No 363 is Palacio de Torre Tagle (see p31). Carry on to pedestrianised Jirón de la Unión and turn left, walking one block south.

6 Iglesia de la Merced

The original La Merced was built on the site of Lima's first Mass in 1534, although the present structure dates back to the 18th century.

Continue south down busy Jirón de la Unión for three more blocks.

7 Plaza San Martín

Finish off with a well-deserved Pisco Sour or a cream tea on the terrace of the 1920s Gran Hotel Bolívar.

Open: 9.30am–5pm. Admission charge.

Walk: Lima – through 500 years of history

LIMA BY THE SEA

The upmarket *barrios* (neighbourhoods) of Miraflores and Barranco are a world away from Lima's historic centre. Miraflores is a modern enclave, with boutiques, fine dining and sophisticated hotels, but it is also the site of Huaca Pucllana, an important Inca temple. Barranco is a residential seaside district of mostly dilapidated 19th-century houses that has attracted many artists, giving it a distinctly bohemian feel.

Barranco

Known for its bars and nightclubs, Barranco is relaxed by day, with the atmosphere of a small town. This mostly residential area has several interesting museums and attractive seaside walks. Consider visiting these places in the afternoon, and staying on in the evening for dinner, drinking and even dancing.

Museo de Electricidad (Museum of Electricity)

An old red tram car called Breda takes tourists on a three-block ride down Avenida Pedro de Osma. It leaves from the tiny Museum of Electricity, which shows old photos of Lima's historic electrical trams.
Avenida Pedro de Osma 105. Tel/fax: (01) 477 6577. http://museoelectri.perucultural.org.pe. Open: 10am–5pm. Admission charge.

Museo-Galeria Arte Popular de Ayacucho

Colourful folk-art figures from the Andean region of Ayacucho as well as some fascinating portable altars that were used by rural priests are displayed here.
Avenida Pedro de Osma 116. Tel/fax: (01) 247 0599. Open: Mon–Sat 9am–5pm. Free admission.

Museo Pedro de Osma

This museum has an interesting private collection of colonial art from between the 17th and the 19th centuries, including paintings, mostly from the Cusqueña School, sculpture, silverware and furniture. It is housed in an exquisite, century-old mansion that is arguably the main attraction.
Avenida Pedro de Osma 423. Tel: (01) 467 0141. www.museopedrodeosma.org. Open: Thur–Sun 10am–6pm. Admission charge.

Puente de Suspiros (Bridge of Sighs)

This is a small bridge built in the late 1800s that offers pleasant views out to sea, with a walkway down to the beach.

Miraflores

With its gardens and roads fanning out to the sea, Miraflores is, quite literally, a breath of fresh air after Lima's city centre. This is where most of the best hotels, restaurants and shops are found, making it a great place to wander, eat and shop.

Handicrafts markets

Avenida Petit Thouars (particularly the section from Ricardo Palma to General Vidal) is lined with markets selling souvenirs and handicrafts, such as textiles, jewellery and handmade alpaca sweaters from around the country. Mercado Indio, also known as the Artisans' Market, at No 5245 (corner with General Vidal) is definitely the best, but also try Artesanía Expo Inti at No 5495.

All markets closed: Sun.

Huaca Pucllana

This pre-Inca site dates back to between AD 200 and 700. It is made up of both ceremonial and administrative sections, with the *huaca* (temple), a large mud-brick pyramid more than 20m (66ft) high.

Avenida General Borgoño, Cdra 8. Tel: (01) 445 8695. http://pucllana.perucultural.org.pe (Spanish only). Open: Wed–Mon 9am–4pm. Free admission.

Parque del Amor

This Park of Love, forming landscaped gardens on cliffs overlooking the Pacific Ocean, is prettier than Miraflores' Parque Central. Benches decorated with tiles feature romantic phrases, and in the centre is a huge monument of an embracing couple, *El Beso* (*The Kiss*), by local sculptor Victor Delfin. It was opened on St Valentine's Day in 1993, and romantics come here to catch the sunset and compete for the longest kiss.

Malecón Cisneros. Open: 6am–midnight. Free admission.

The Parque del Amor in Miraflores is a rare monument to love, instead of war

Lima, Nazca and the south coast

Colonial country

From 1528, when the Spanish first traded with natives from the Pacific city of Tumbes, the Incas' empire quickly crumbled. Within a few short years, they were defeated by a combination of brute force and disease, though simmering discontent among Inca subjects also played its part. Spanish rule spread quickly, with the conquerors cleverly adapting existing social structures for their own gain.

Ornate religious art was used to impress the natives

Carving up the country

The conquerors established coastal cities such as Lima and Trujillo to ferry gold and silver back to the Spanish king; this loot was transported on mules from all over South America. As disease killed more and more natives, additional towns were built to consolidate the remaining rural stragglers into manageable workforces. The countryside was carved up into quasi-feudal *encomiendas*, and later *haciendas*, which paid huge tributes to the Spanish Crown – a bone of contention in the independence struggles that were to come.

For financial gain

Under the Incas, natural resources were carefully managed, but the Spanish stripped the land bare, robbing the people of farmland and mineral wealth. The native people were used for cheap, hard labour, fiercely controlled and heavily taxed. The colonists' barbarism has been extensively documented, though what is often forgotten is that the Incas themselves subjugated entire peoples solely for their own benefit.

Art and architecture

The colonists brought Christianity to a pagan people who worshipped the sun and moon. Spanish cathedrals were built on Inca temples, with art and architecture forming part of the crusade, but native religion adapted. The Incas' Mother Earth, Pachamama, became the Virgin Mary, their creator Sun God, Christ.

Besides the churches, elaborate mansions and municipal buildings were constructed in places such as Lima, Arequipa, Ayacucho, Cuzco and Trujillo – many of which can still be seen today.

An independent nation

Despite 300 years of Spanish rule, which ended only in 1821, the spirit of the native people was not extinguished. Today, Quechua, the Amerindian language, is, along with Spanish, an official language, and Aymara is still spoken by the people of the same name who live in the Andes. Just under half of the current population is indigenous, around 40 per cent are *mestizo* (a mix of Spanish and Peruvian), 15 per cent are European, and the rest are mostly Japanese, Chinese and African – the latter brought in as slave labour when the Indian population dwindled. Peru's folklore traditions are still strong, and native culture today far outshines the

Lima's grand colonial architecture

Spanish legacy – it is Machu Picchu, not colonial Lima, that visitors really come to see.

HEALTHY CONCERN

The Spanish did not intend to exterminate the native Peruvian population; after all, they were useful labour. However, simple diseases such as smallpox, measles and flu, brought in by the Europeans, contributed in killing off a staggering 90 per cent of the population in the mid-16th century – far more than were killed in colonial wars or through exploitation.

THE NAZCA LINES

Etched in the barren desert as if they are a message to the gods (or some say to outer space), the Nazca Lines are enormous geoglyphs created by the Nazca people between 200 BC and AD 600. The 300 or so shapes form animals such as a giant hummingbird and a massive monkey with a spiralling tail, and flowers and even an astronaut. Some of the geometric patterns are 300m (984ft) across, and together they cover an area of more than 500sq km (193sq miles).

Despite constant study and many imaginative theories, no one knows for sure why the Nazca Lines were formed. They are extraordinary, with an almost spiritual quality, and the mystery only adds to their appeal. It is known that the forms were 'drawn' by removing the dark iron oxide-covered stones that are scattered through the desert, leaving a light contrasting colour behind. The stones that are left stop the underlying soil from blowing over and blurring the lines, while the desert climate means there is little rainfall to wash them away.

The lines were discovered only in 1927 when seen by chance from a commercial plane. When the American Professor Paul Kosok began to study them, he assumed at first that they were some kind of irrigation system, but quickly went on to call them 'the biggest astronomy book of the world'. In the late 1960s, Erich von Däniken briefly argued in *Chariots of the Gods* that the lines were an ancient landing strip for extraterrestrials.

By this time, Maria Reiche, a German-born mathematician and archaeologist, had already brought the Nazca Lines to the attention of the world. Reiche studied the lines from the 1940s until she died in 1998. Although she couldn't prove conclusively that the Nazca Lines were an astronomical calendar, it seems likely that such a monumental gesture was part of some religious purpose. They were probably an enormous visual prayer to the gods – asking for water in the desert, fish in the sea, and

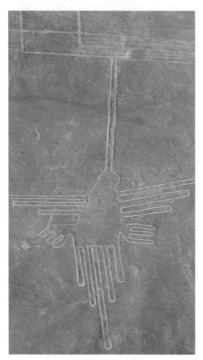

The enigmatic 'Hummingbird' seen from the sky

This figure has been nickmaned 'the Spaceman'

crops to grow – as well as a statement of identity, like the pyramids in Egypt.

It is possible to see some of the figures from the Mirador, a viewing platform on the side of the Pan-American Highway, but the only real way to see the Nazca Lines is from the air. The 45-minute flight can be arranged on the day through a number of different companies. Alternatively, take a one- or two-day bus tour from Lima.

Casa-Museo Maria Reiche

This outstanding museum is named after the archaeologist Maria Reiche, who lived most of her life in this house. It displays information not just on the Nazca Lines, with access to several of the figures, but also on important archaeological pieces from the Paracas, Ica and Inca cultures. *Panamericana Km 418, San Pedro. Tel: (01) 522 379. Open: 9am–5pm. Admission charge.*

Chauchilla

Southwest of Nazca on the Pan-American Highway, Chauchilla is an interesting pre-Inca cemetery, although it has been the victim of grave robbers (*see p45*).

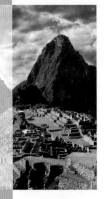

Excursion: The Ballestas Islands

This group of sun-kissed islands, 240km (150 miles) south of Lima, is one of the best places to see wildlife in the whole of Peru, and indeed they are known as the Baby Galápagos Islands (the Galápagos are only 400km/248 miles to the north). The region is also important historically. It was here that the liberator General San Martín landed in 1821 to free Peru from the Spanish.

Erosion by the sea has formed numerous spectacular arches and caves on these islands, where thousands of birds and sea lions shelter. In fact, the islands get their name from *ballestas*, meaning 'archery bows'. More than 150 species of marine birds, including pelicans, cormorants and Humboldt penguins, can be seen, although the penguins in particular can be somewhat elusive. The red and white flamingoes found here are thought to have been the inspiration for the colours of the independence flag designed by General San Martín.

Boat trips to Ballestas

Tours, which include a ride on a motorboat with a guide, leave from El Chaco jetty in Paracas at 8am and 10am and take around two hours. Most visitors choose to stay overnight in Pisco first, where either the town's hotels or travel agencies can make all necessary arrangements for a visit to the islands. Dress warmly, bring a hat for protection from all those bird droppings, and be prepared for the terrible stench they can create. In the mid-19th century, this region produced large amounts of guano (bird droppings), which was exported to Europe to be used as a fertiliser. For a long time, this was Peru's most important industry.

On the way out, through the choppy blue waters, at Punta Pejerry you will see *El Candelabro* – an enormous 'candelabra' etched into the desert

Birdlife on the Ballestas Islands

A relaxed seal poses for the camera

hillside. Theories regarding its origin abound. Some experts link it with the Chavín culture; others say it was a 'road sign' for pirates. Landing on the islands is forbidden in order to protect the wildlife, but some boats will sail close to the land – even this disrupts the fragile environment and shouldn't be encouraged. You may see female sea lions following your boat, while their males lie nonchalantly on the rocks. Flamingoes can be spotted in the southern section of the bay, although there is normally an extra charge to go this far.

Back on dry land, have lunch in Paracas and hire a taxi for half a day to return to Lima in the afternoon. Alternatively, continue with a tour of the Paracas Nature Reserve, which can be combined with the Ballestas trip to make a full-day excursion.

Paracas National Reserve

The reserve, 15km (9½ miles) south of Pisco, was set up in 1975 to protect wildlife both on the land and in the sea. Just outside the village of Paracas, there is an obelisk commemorating the landing of liberator General José de San Martín. A couple of kilometres (1¼ miles) inside the park is a small museum, Museo J C Tello, with displays of local textiles and skulls. From here, it's a short walk down to the bay where birds, including flamingoes, can be seen feeding at the water's edge. Dirt roads lead over the peninsula to the fishing village of Lagunillas, 6km (3¾ miles) away, and another 6km (3¾ miles) on to El Mirador de Lobos (Wolf Lookout) on the cliffs. Here there are sweeping views and La Catedral, a towering rock formation.
Open: 9am–5pm. Admission charge.

Drive: Coast and desert

This drive takes in important centres for wildlife and wine, as well as some spectacular archaeological sites and a magical oasis. The route follows the Panamericana (Pan-American Highway), Peru's best road, making it almost impossible to get lost. The whole drive down to Nazca, 450km (280 miles) from Lima, can be done in a day. However, taking in all the sights along the way, including the Ballestas Islands (see p42) by boat and the Nazca Lines (see p40) by plane, will take three to four days.

1 Pucusana

This traditional fishing village, 68km (42 miles) south of Lima, is a pleasant place to stop for an hour or two. Explore the beach of Naplo, hire a boat to the cave called El Boquerón del Diablo (The Devil's Mouth), and enjoy a lunch of delicious local seafood.

Continue for another 172km (107 miles) south along the Pan-American Highway, passing through the town of San Vicente de Cañete a little over halfway, and then on to Chincha Alta, both centres for wine growing.

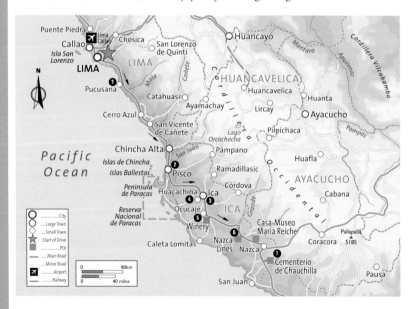

Huacachina is a real oasis in the desert

2 Pisco

This coastal city is part port and part colonial centre. Half a day's drive south of Lima, it is a world away from the capital and home to the grape alcohol that is Peru's national drink (*see p46*). A monument to General José de San Martín stands in Plaza de Armas, and nearby is Club Social Pisco, the general's original headquarters. Pisco is the ideal jumping-off point for the Ballestas Islands and the Paracas National Reserve (*see p43*).
Drive south on the Panamericana for a further 80km (50 miles). From Pisco, the road turns sharply inland, rising gently to the hilltop town of Ica.

3 Ica

Ica is worth a stop for its impressive regional museum, pretty colonial churches and nearby *bodegas* (wineries).
Drive 5km (3 miles) due west of Ica to Huacachina.

4 Huacachina

This beautiful oasis surrounded by enormous sand dunes and attractive palm trees is best avoided in the heat of the midday sun. Cool off with a swim in the lake, or hire a dune-surfing board from a nearby restaurant.
Return to Ica and drive south for 40km (25 miles) to the Ocucaje bodega.

5 Ocucaje

At the Ocucaje *bodega* in the centre of the town of the same name, you can take a tour and buy locally made wine and Pisco.
Avenida Principal. Tel: (056) 40 8011. www.ocucaje.com. Open: Mon–Fri 9am–noon & 2–5pm. Admission charge. Drive southeast for 80km (50 miles) along the Panamericana to the town of Nazca.

6 Nazca Lines

Flights take off from an airfield on the edge of Nazca over the Nazca Lines, 12km (7½ miles) away (*see p40*).
Drive about 20km (12½ miles) south along the Panamericana, and then 12km (7½ miles) east along a dirt road to the Cementerio de Chauchilla.

7 Cementerio de Chauchilla (Chauchilla Cemetery)

This pre-Inca site includes ancient mummies and artefacts in their graves, dating back to AD 1000.
No telephone. Open: 8am–5pm. Admission charge. Head back to Nazca and stay the night before continuing on to your next destination.

Drive: Coast and desert

Pisco: more sweet than sour

Pisco Sour, Peru's national drink, is served in every restaurant in the country, as well as in many others throughout the world. Although Chileans will tell you that the grape brandy belongs to them, it's generally agreed that pisco is as Peruvian as Machu Picchu. The drink is said to take its name from the city of Pisco (see p45), whose surrounding fertile valleys are ideal for the cultivation of the pisco grape. The famous cocktail made with the powerful alcohol is tart rather than sour, usually bringing a smile to all who try it.

A piece of pisco history

Soon after the Spanish invaded Peru, they began bringing grape vines over from the Canary Islands in an attempt to establish wine production. Peruvian wine became so popular in Spain, at the expense of domestic production, that the export trade was banned in 1614. A by-product of the ban was that the Peruvians concentrated on making the local grape brandy instead, and the spirit gained in popularity in the 17th and 18th centuries. It was drunk mostly by sailors who ordered 'pisco', named after the port where it was

RECIPE FOR PISCO SOUR

1 egg white
1 tbsp sugar
1 glass of pisco
Juice from six limes (or lemons)
Crushed ice
Angostura bitters
Cinnamon

First beat the egg white and sugar together in a blender. Then add the pisco, lime juice, ice and angostura bitters. Mix together, pour into glasses, sprinkle with cinnamon, and enjoy this refreshing, frothy drink.

purchased. However, the name of the drink may also originate from the Quechua word for 'bird' (pisqu), or from the old clay vessels called piskos in which the firewater was stored.

Sour grapes

Pisco is made from grapes grown in the rich soils of the Ica Valley, around 300km (186 miles) south of Lima, which are watered by the Pisco and Ica rivers. There are actually four recognised varieties of pisco, categorised by the grape used in production:

Acholado or 'half-breed' is the pisco produced from mixing aromatic grapes, such as Moscatel, and non-aromatic grapes, like Quebranta.

Aromatic is the result of the

distillation of grapes such as Moscatel and Italia.

Mosto Verde or 'Green Must' is distilled from unfermented grape juice.

Pure is made from the non-aromatic black grape Quebranta, brought over from Spain, and sometimes from other non-aromatic grapes such as Mollar and Nera Corriente.

In celebration of pisco

Ica holds an annual pisco and wine festival, the Festival de la Vendimia, in the second week of March, when the grapes are harvested. Apart from parades, parties and general merriment, the Queen of the Festival leads a beauty pageant in which she, along with her attractive assistants, treads grapes in an enormous vat. National Pisco Sour Day is celebrated enthusiastically on the first Saturday in February. Cities around Peru mark this decidedly frivolous event in different ways. In Lima, marketing executives raise a glass to increasing international exports, while others make patriotic attempts to break the world record for drinking Pisco Sours.

At the heart of every good Pisco Sour is the famous grape brandy, a clear-coloured but lethal spirit

The central Andes

Visitors to Peru are inevitably drawn towards the Andes. This is the world's longest mountain range, with 100 peaks rising 6,000m (19,700ft) or more. Huaraz, 450km (280 miles) from Lima, is 3km (1¾ miles) above sea level; this city of 100,000 people is higher than many European ski resorts. The valley around it, the Callejón de Huaylas, is bordered by the Cordillera Negra to the west. To the east, the snowcapped Cordillera Blanca boasts Peru's highest peak, Huascarán (6,768m/22,206ft).

Almost the entire Blanca range has been a protected national park since 1975, and was declared a UNESCO World Heritage Site ten years later. Trekkers come here

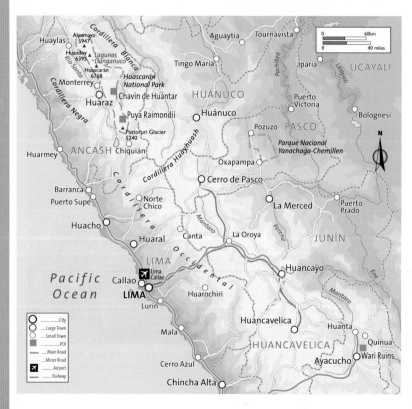

Cordillera Blanca

Huaylas · Alpamayo 5947

Huandoy 6395 ▲ Lagunas Llanganuco

Rio Santa

Huascarán 6768 · *Huascarán National Park*

Monterrey

Cordillera Negra

Huaraz · Chavin de Huántar

Puya Raimondii

▲ Pastoruri Glacier 5240

Huarmey · ANCASH · Chiquián

Cordillera Huayhuash

Barranca

Puerto Supe

Norte Chico

Cordillera Occidental

Huacho

Huaral · Canta

Mantaro

Pacific Ocean

Callao · Lima Callao ✈

LIMA

Lurin

Mala

Cerro Azul

Chincha Alta

Aguaytia · Tournavista

Pachitea

Iparia · UCAYALI

Ucayali

Tingo Maria

HUÁNUCO

Puerto Victoria

Puya Raimondii · Huánuco · Bolognesi

Pozuzo · PASCO

Parque Nacional Yanachaga-Chemillén

Oxapampa

Cerro de Pasco

La Merced · Puerto Prado

La Oroya · Perene

JUNÍN

Huancayo

Huarochiri · Mantaro

Ene

Huancavelica · Huanta

HUANCAVELICA · Quinua

Ayacucho · Wari Ruins

0 — 60km
0 — 40 miles

N

○ ....City
○ ....Large Town
○ ....Small Town
■ ....POI
— ....Main Road
— ....Minor Road
✈ ....Airport
........Railway

The snowy peaks of the Cordillera Blanca in the central Andes

from all over the world to marvel at the crystal-clear lakes, unique plant and animal life, and the majestic glacial peaks that loom above. On the eastern side of the Huascarán National Park is the archaeological treasure Chavín de Huántar, recognised as one of the cradles of South American civilisation. For the adventurous, the Río Santa, which drains the Blanca range towards the Pacific, offers breathtaking opportunities for Class IV white-water rafting.

South of the Blanca range is the Cordillera Huayhuash. It is smaller and less visited than the Blanca, and the trekking here is generally more challenging, but it affords some of the most spectacular mountain scenery anywhere in the world. Once a Shining Path guerrilla zone, it is now informally policed by representatives of the local communities and is generally safe (*see p123*).

The larger of the Lagunas Llanganuco in the Huascarán National Park

HUASCARÁN AND THE CORDILLERA BLANCA

Travellers cannot fail to be impressed by the Cordillera Blanca. There are 50 peaks here, the highest of which, Huascarán, gives its name to the national park. Perhaps the most awe-inspiring of all the summits is Alpamayo (5,947m/19,512ft), an almost perfect snow-topped pyramid that appears on countless Peruvian postcards. Of course, the area is a mountaineer's paradise, but there are trekking opportunities for all levels of ability, and trips can be as short as one day, although acclimatisation beforehand is a must (*see opposite*).

Huaraz

Most travellers stop in this city, a day's drive from Lima, to kit up and prepare for high-altitude trekking. There are plenty of supermarkets to choose from, but the bustling market is more interesting and fun, offering the same food but at cheaper prices. *Benzina blanca* (camping gas) can be purchased from any of the small *ferreterías* (hardware stores) around the city, though it may need filtering before use. Huaraz is also the place to hire *arrieros* (guides) and *burros* (mules) if you are planning an extended trip.

Huascarán National Park

As well as some of the world's highest mountains, this 3,400sq km (1,313sq mile) ecological reserve counts 296 lakes and 41 rivers within its boundaries. In this valuable habitat, home to the Andean condor and the spectacled bear, there are

ALTITUDE SICKNESS

At an altitude of 3,000m (10,000ft), there is only 70 per cent of the oxygen available at sea level, and the air gets even thinner higher up. Rapid ascent, exertion and excessive time spent above this height can all lead to altitude sickness. Symptoms include nausea, sleepless nights and headaches. It can affect even experienced climbers, so don't be complacent. There are prescription drugs (often with side effects) and herbs (notably ginkgo biloba) that may help, but the best prevention is to spend two or three days at 3,000m (10,000ft) before slowly ascending. Stick to a high carbohydrate diet, avoid alcohol and tobacco, and stay hydrated.

around 800 plant species, including the astonishing *Puya raimondii*, found mainly on Nevada Pastoruri (*see right*). There are plenty of well-established routes, guides can be hired in Huaraz, and treks can be combined with stints of rafting, horse-riding and mountain biking. The small admission charge supports park maintenance and scientific study. *http://whc.unesco.org/en/list/333. Admission charge.*

Lagunas Llanganuco

Nestling in the valley formed by Huascarán and Huandoy (6,160m/20,211ft) is a pair of dazzling turquoise lakes known as Lagunas Llanganuco (3,800m/12,468ft), a popular Huaraz day trip and camping point for Blanca trekkers with spectacular mountain views. Aim to get here before 1pm, when the lakes' reflections are at their most dramatic.

Monterrey

A day trip to the thermal springs here, only 5km (3 miles) north of Huaraz, is a gentle introduction to hiking at altitude, and a bathe alfresco in the warm waters is a wonderful, relaxing experience that will soothe those aching muscles.
Springs open: 8am–6pm. Admission charge.

Pastoruri Glacier

A visit to this ice-packed peak (5,240m/17,192ft) is manageable as a day trip from Huaraz or as part of a longer excursion. On the way, there is a chance to see the rare *Puya raimondii*. The 3m (10ft) tall rosette is spectacular enough, but as it nears the end of its life (anywhere from 30 to 100 years) it flowers for the first and only time and sprouts a bloom that is almost three storeys high.

The glacial peak of Pastoruri

Excursion: Chavín de Huántar

Between the Amazon and the eastern slopes of the Cordillera Blanca, an important trading and cultural centre was founded in 800 BC by the Chavín people. The Chavíns did not communicate through writing, but they produced intricate metalwork, stone carvings and ceramics enlivened with complex contours that transmitted hidden meanings between their high priests.

Getting there

The ruins of Chavín de Huántar can be visited on a day trip from Huaraz, and many travellers seize this opportunity while getting used to the high altitude of the region. A plethora of companies in the city offer organised tours, with trips usually leaving early in the morning to arrive at the ruins around midday. Visitors arriving independently should seek out one of the knowledgeable guides frequenting the ruins.

La Plaza Circular

The plaza is surrounded by hills on all sides. If one stood in its centre and looked towards the smaller of the two visible staircases, the winter solstice sunrise would have appeared directly above the hill beyond.

El Templo Antiguo (The Old Temple)

Like many sites, Huántar shows evidence of buildings from different stages of development. The Old Temple dates back to around 900 BC, and is a classic form of the Initial Period – so called because it was when ceramics initially appeared in Peruvian culture. A large pyramid-shaped mound was constructed and a flat plaza cleared in front of it. The larger set of steps that is still visible belonged to the mound of the Old Temple and led to the temple's entrance, which would have been brightly decorated.

La Galería del Lanzón

Walk deep in the heart of the Old Temple, through the low narrow passageway, and the stone sculpture of Lanzón, the Chavíns' supreme god, suddenly appears from the gloom.

El Templo Nuevo (The New Temple)

When the New Temple was built some 400 years after the old, it was on a larger scale with a square plaza southeast of the old circular one, and a *castillo* (platform) incorporating the old mound. Secret passages and stairways would allow the high priests to appear on the *castillo* as if by magic.

Las Falcónidas (The Falcons)

The stairs to the platform are lost, but the entrance gate has been reassembled. The left side is white granite, with black limestone on the right, and the columns are decorated with mythical bird-cat creatures resembling the monochrome falcon.

La Galería Doble Mensula

A steep staircase leads to this extensive and labyrinthine gallery. The passages here are wider, thanks to the *doble mensula* (double cantilevered) roof structure. A walk through these passages can be spookily atmospheric – especially if the lighting fails, so bring a torch.

A statue of Lanzón, the Chavín supreme god

AYACUCHO AND THE CENTRAL HIGHLANDS

The central highlands of Peru are rich in indigenous culture and colonial tradition, yet the area is only now beginning to be discovered by travellers, partly because of its remoteness, but also because of years of Shining Path rebel activity. Now, the region is considered safe, and Ayacucho in particular is a fascinating destination, with dozens of churches and colonial mansions in the historic city centre, a thriving arts and crafts industry, and pre-Columbian ruins nearby. L C Busre operates daily two-hour flights to Ayacucho from Lima, and Aerocondor flies three times a week. The road from Lima, via Pisco, is also spectacular.

Characteristic crafts of Ayacucho

Churches

Ayacucho has dozens of churches, the most beautiful of which are La Catedral (1612) in the main square, San Francisco de Asis (1552), Santo Domingo (1548) and La Compañía (1605). Most open for early-morning Mass, except in the week before Easter when all-day opening is the norm. Then, religious pilgrims gather here for the Masses and processions of Holy Week, culminating in huge parties on Good Friday and Easter Saturday.

Museo Andres Cáceres

Born in Ayacucho, Andres Cáceres became a hero for leading the Peruvian resistance against Chile in the War of the Pacific. His home is now a museum containing correspondence, photographs and weapons.
Casona Vivanco, 28 de Julio 508, Ayacucho. Tel: (066) 836 166. Open: Mon–Sat 9am–1pm & 3–6pm. Admission charge.

Museo de Arte Popular

During the presidency (1968–75) of the left-leaning Juan Velasco, most of the colonial mansions around the Plaza de Armas were expropriated by the government and are now banks and government offices that can be visited by the public. The exquisite Casona Chacón is now the Banco de Crédito, with some rooms given over to this fascinating museum that documents the history and skills of the townspeople through photographs,

The Quinua monument commemorates a key independence battle

sculpture and crafts displays.
Plaza de Armas, Ayacucho. Tel: (066) 812 467. Open: Tue–Sat 10am–5pm. Free admission.

Museo Histórico Regional de Ayacucho

Housing a collection of weavings by local artisans, and remains from the Inca and Wari periods, this museum is worth a visit for those interested in the archaeology of the region.
Complejo Cultural Simón Bolívar, Independencia, Ayacucho. Tel: (066) 912 360. Open: Mon–Fri 9am–1pm & 3–5pm. Admission charge.

Quinua and the Wari Ruins

Only 22km (13½ miles) from Ayacucho are the remains of the Wari Empire's capital city, once home to 50,000 people. Forerunners of the Inca by 500 years, the Wari dominated the central highlands from here, and, although much of the site is buried, some of the 12m (40ft) high city walls are still visible. Another 15km (9½ miles) north is the town of Quinua, where the Spanish finally surrendered to Peruvian independence fighters after a ferocious battle in 1824. There is a towering white monument nearby to commemorate the event, but of more interest are the fine ceramics for sale by local craftspeople. Day trips can be organised by Wari Tours in Ayacucho.
Wari Tours. Lima 138, Ayacucho. Tel: (066) 311 415. Free admission to ruins.

The Shining Path

It is in the central highlands of Peru, in the province of Ayacucho, that this fearsome revolutionary organisation has its roots. Officially known as the Communist Party of Peru, they adopted the snappier name of Sendero Luminoso (Shining Path) to distinguish themselves from the numerous other communist organisations in Peru. Founded in the late 1960s, the organisation started by Abimael Guzmán (*see box*) initially gained support among the poor farmers in the mountains around Ayacucho.

Violent decades

The group's platform was initially peaceful, but in 1980 the leaders met secretly in Ayacucho and declared war on the state. The Sendero Luminoso acted as a peasants' revenge force, torturing and killing cattle rustlers, unpopular farm managers and criminals – acts that increased their popularity among some sections of the rural population.

Eventually, the government started to take notice. In 1982, emergency powers were granted to the army in the Ayacucho region. Whole villages suspected of supporting the Shining Path were detained, and there were army-sanctioned civilian massacres. For its part, the Shining Path was no less ruthless. One of the worst atrocities occurred in 1992, when two car bombs in the upmarket Lima suburb of Miraflores killed 22 people and left buildings in ruins.

Losing support, gaining enemies

As the Shining Path took over greater and greater areas of the countryside, the farmers who had initially supported them turned against their extremist ways. The group's ideology prevented farmers selling their produce at 'capitalist' markets,

PERU'S CHAIRMAN MAO

The founder of the Shining Path, Abimael Guzmán Reynoso, cast himself as a leader of Peru's downtrodden *campesinos* (farm workers), but Guzmán himself was no farmer. After completing degrees in law and philosophy, he took a job as Professor of Philosophy at Huamanga University in Ayacucho, and became active in left-wing political circles. Guzmán became determined to overthrow the state, destroy bourgeois society and lead a Marxist-Leninist revolution like that spearheaded by Mao Zedong in China. Guzmán attained a cult-like status among his followers, but since his capture in 1992 his influence over Peru's affairs has waned, and he faces a lifetime behind bars.

and their ever more extreme tactics were regarded with horror. The organisation also targeted individuals, not just government figures but also peasants' and workers' leaders, as they tried to win support through fear and intimidation.

In areas like Ayacucho, the Peruvian government set up armed 'self-defence committees', whose members were essentially anyone willing to oppose the Shining Path. These self-defence groups, though also guilty of human-rights abuses, severely weakened the rebels, and the killer blow was the capture of the charismatic Guzmán. With the leader in custody, the group soon fell apart, and attacks became less and less frequent.

The country has paid a bloody price. Almost 70,000 people died, half at the hands of the Shining Path, with government forces and other groups responsible for the rest. Thankfully, Peru seems to be trying to put its bloody and harrowing recent past behind it, and the central highlands, once the stronghold of the Marxists, is now a more peaceful area.

Ayacucho, once a Shining Path stronghold, is rediscovering its colonial past

Cusco and Machu Picchu

The Incas called their domain Tawantinsuyo (Four Quarters of the Earth) and it stretched from Colombia in the north to Chile in the south. All commands came from the hub of Cusco (which translates literally as 'belly button'), and devotees from the Four Quarters thronged to worship in its temples. Today, the city is the focal point for tourists to Peru, and the departure point for the magnificent Machu Picchu. Although this is a remote area, deep in the Andes, it is only a one-hour flight from Lima.

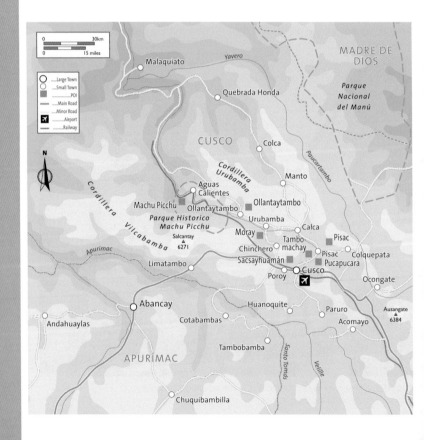

Cusco is almost every traveller's favourite destination in Peru. Not only does it have layer upon layer of history, but it is also a lovely relaxing place with excellent facilities. There are charming hotels, diverse restaurants and lively all-night bars, as well as varied shopping in the local markets, galleries and souvenir shops. The historic city centre, where llamas stroll the streets, can be explored by gentle wandering. Alternatively, take a walking tour (*see p62*), visiting many of the more interesting sights.

The Sacred Valley is dotted with traditional villages, including Pisac with its famous Sunday market, which is a magnet for locals and tourists alike. Reach the breathtaking Inca stronghold of Machu Picchu by hiking the famous trail (there is a mini version for those who can't face the full four days), or travel by train and give your feet a rest.

Many tourists fly in and out of Cusco, spending just a day or two in the city and another on a trip to Machu Picchu. Take time to savour the delights of this area; even those who do not get excited about history find themselves thrilled by this mountain citadel. If you are seeking an adrenaline fix, or just a change of perspective, you can shoot down rapid-filled rivers on rafts, whizz down mountain passes on bicycles and trot around ancient temples on horseback.

Cusco centre

It is thought that in the early 1400s the ninth Inca, Pachucutec, designed Cusco in the shape of a sacred puma. Fortified Sacsayhuamán formed its tooth-filled head while Coricancha, the Temple of the Sun, represented the loins. The heart of the puma was Huacapata, a ceremonial square where the Plaza de Armas now stands. Four main roads radiated from here to each corner of the far-reaching Inca Empire.

The Spanish destroyed many of the Inca monuments in Cusco's centre, building their churches on the old foundations, although ironically a major earthquake in 1650 then

Cusco and Machu Picchu

Cusco centre with the main square in the foreground

flattened many of the colonial buildings. As a result, Cusco is a rich mix of colonial splendour and Inca remains. The centre is best explored on foot (*see p62*).

La Catedral

It took no less than 100 years (beginning in 1559) to build this impressive building that is flanked on the right by the church of El Triunfo, Cusco's oldest church built in 1536, and on the left by the church of Jesús María (1733). The cathedral is famed for its paintings from the Cusco School, such as *The Last Supper* by Marcos Zapata. Note too the wonderful wooden altar and decorative side chapels.

INSIDER INFORMATION

Buy the excellent-value 'tourist ticket' – the *Boleto Turístico* – that allows entry to many major sights in the city and several in the surrounding area. It can be bought at the Oficina Ejecutiva del Comité (OFEC) (*Avenida Sol 103, Cusco. Tel. (084) 227 037*). If you buy a tour from any of the travel agencies in the city, the ticket price is normally included. Note that opening times for all sights tend to be somewhat erratic.

North side of Plaza de Armas. Open: 10am–6pm. Admission charge.

La Compañía

Work on the ornate Baroque-fronted Jesuit church began in 1571. The building was reconstructed after being

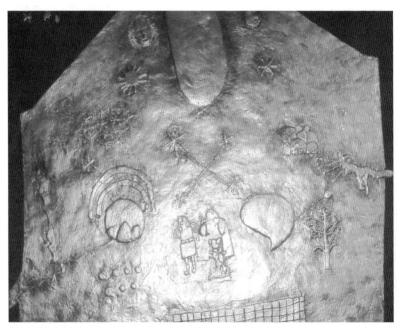

A wall of gold depicting the Inca world in Cusco's Templo de Coricancha

The Baroque façade of La Compañía

completely destroyed in the 1650 earthquake. Because it looked as if the church would outshine the cathedral's splendour, the pope intervened – but too late.

Southeastern side of Plaza de Armas. Open: Irregular hours. Free admission.

Iglesia y Convento de La Merced

Cusco's third-most-important church was another of the many victims of the 1650 earthquake. The complex includes beautiful white stone cloisters with a peaceful garden, and a small exhibition museum of Cusquena paintings. Don't miss the solid gold monstrance covered in hundreds of diamonds and pearls.

Mantas 121 (southwest side of the Plaza San Francisco). Monastery and museum open: 8am–12.30pm & 2–5.30pm. Admission charge.

San Blas

The artisans' quarter is crossed with pretty narrow streets in Spanish style, with flower-filled courtyards and balconies. Shops sell locally crafted pottery, paintings, textiles and stonework, and there are also plenty of cosmopolitan bars and restaurants. In its centre is San Blas Plazoleta, where 49 gargoyles guard a fountain in the shape of a *chakana*, the Inca cross whose 12 corners represent the months of the year. Here, too, the Iglesia San Blas is worth a look inside for its exquisitely carved wooden pulpit dating from the 17th century.

Walk: Around Cusco

This walk focuses on Cusco's museums and churches, but there are also many pedestrian streets that you can wander down and find yourself in another century. Here, look out for the original Inca stonework at the bases of houses, shaming the rough masonary above.

This walk takes half a day and covers 2km (1¼ miles), allowing time to see the sights.

Start at the Plaza de Armas.

1 Plaza de Armas

This sloping main square is at the heart of Cusco, which was in its time the 'navel' of the enormous Inca Empire. In recent years, Quechua street signs have been added to the Spanish, so that, for example, the Plaza de Armas is also known as Haukaypata. Here, explore the cathedral and the church of La Compañía *(see p60)*.

Walk uphill along Cuesta del Almirante (to the left of the cathedral as you are facing it) to Museo Inka on your left.

2 Museo Inka

A significant collection of Inca artefacts is housed in this admiral's palace.
Cuesta del Almirante 103. Open: Mon–Fri 8am–6pm, Sat 9am–4pm. Admission charge.
Continue up the hill to the pretty little square of Plazolata de Nazarenas and turn left.

3 Museo de Arte Precolombino

The newest and very slick addition to Cusco's museums is a real find, showing pre-Columbian art from the 13th to 16th centuries in a 17th-century convent. Have dinner or a cocktail in the sophisticated MAP café inside.
Plazolata de Nazarenas 231.
Tel: (084) 233 210. Open: 9am–5pm. Admission charge.

Map

```
0        100 metres          ★ ....Start of Walk
0        100 yards           🕇 ....Cathedral
                             🛈 ....Information

N

        Museo
        de Arte
        Precolombino
           PLAZOLATA DE              Iglesia
           NAZARENAS    SAN BLAS     San Blas
                        PLAZOLETA
   Museo                HATUN
   Inka
           La                Museo de Arte
           Catedral          Religioso del
        🕇                   Arzobispado
           EL TRIUNFO
  PLAZA
  DE ARMAS     El Triunfo
        ★
                    SANTA
                    MONICA
              Convento y Museo
              Santa Catalina
  La Compañía
  Iglesia y        Craft
  Convento         Market
  de La Merced
        🛈
                 PLAZOLETA
                 SANTO
                 DOMINGO
                      Templo de
                      Coricancha &
                      Museo
                      Arqueológico
```

Walk back through the Plazolata and one block along Palacio San Augustín to the corner with Hatunrumiyoc, where you will find the Museo de Arte Religioso del Arzobispado.

4 Museo de Arte Religioso del Arzobispado

Religious art is housed in this old archbishop's palace that was once the palace of Inca Roca's. Fitted into one of the original Inca walls outside is a magnificent 12-angled stone.
Hatunrumiyoc and Herejes.
Tel: (084) 222 781. Open: Mon–Sat 9am–12.30pm & 3–6pm.
Admission charge.
Turn right out of the museum up the steep cobblestone street of Hatunrumiyoc to Cuesta de San Blas.

5 Iglesia San Blas

Galleries line the walk up to the artists' quarter of San Blas with its pretty church (*see p61*). You may want to shop here, or stop for coffee.
Return down Cuesta de San Blas, turning left onto San Augustín, and then right on Zetas. Plazoleta Santo Domingo is on your left.

6 Templo de Coricancha (Temple of the Sun)

This is the most important Inca

At nearly 3,500m (11,434ft), Cusco is one of the highest cities in the world, so take time to acclimatise to avoid altitude sickness.

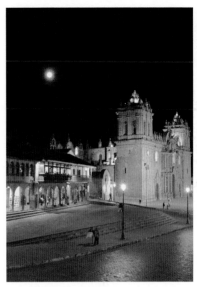

Cusco's Plaza de Armas at night

Walk: Around Cusco

temple in the city, and it once had gem-studded, gold-plated walls (there are replicas inside). These were designed to reflect the sun, which was worshipped here. Walk through the restored esplanade to the Museo Arqueológico del Coricancha.
Plazoleta Santo Domingo. Open: Mon–Sat 8am–5pm, Sun 2–4pm.
Admission charge.
Exit the temple back into Plazoleta Santo Domingo. Cross Zetas and, with the Plazoleta on your right, head up Pampa Castillo. A little further up, Castillo becomes the pedestrian alleyway of Loreto. Pass the small craft market on your left. Finish back at the Plaza de Armas for something to eat at one of the charming restaurant balconies overlooking the square.

The Sacred Valley

Officially, this is the Vilcanota/ Urubamba River valley that spreads north and northwest from Cusco. Dotted with Inca ruins, host to a vibrant Indian market and a number of tranquil, traditional villages, it's a good place to explore or relax. The more adventurous can try rafting down the river (*see p75*). For many of the villagers, life has changed little since the days before the Spanish Conquest in 1532.

You may choose to visit this area independently (there are regular, reasonably reliable bus services from Cusco and car-hire facilities) or to take part in an organised tour. Most people visit this area on a day trip, but there is enough to keep visitors happily occupied for several days.

Sacsayhuamán

The fortress of Sacsayhuamán towers above the main square in Cusco, the white figure of Christ on the top spectacularly illuminated at night, making it a good way to get your bearings. Fifteen kilometres (9^1/2 miles) north of Cusco, the fortress is on the way to the Sacred Valley. Sacsayhuamán (locals pronounce it 'sexy woman' to amuse tourists) is made up of three rows of zigzagged, teeth-like fortifications. It took over 70 years to construct, using enormous 80-tonne (78-ton) stones, which needed 100 men to move them.

Pisac – ruins and market

'Modern' Pisac, lying next to the river, actually dates back to colonial times. The Sunday food and craft market here (*open: 9am–5pm*) is a bustling atmospheric affair, while the Thursday market is smaller and quieter. Tourists are bussed in en masse, but it's not just curious visitors who come to shop here. This is a functioning market, and villagers from the surrounding basin turn up to buy wares, or more likely to barter. Like markets the world over, it is also an excuse to take part in a social event, which in this case includes a Mass and procession from the church.

The Inca part of town sits on a low mountain top, 0.5km (^{1}/3 mile) away. The ruins are reached by a steep 5km (3-mile) walk taking around two hours from the church in Pisac's plaza. Alternatively, drive up the 10km (6-mile) paved road, or even take a taxi. Drink sellers meet climbers at the top. Take time to absorb the scenic gorge with its terracing, and hawks soaring overhead, then explore the fortress temples to the sun and moon and the Inca crosses in the ground.

Ollantaytambo

Like so many Inca constructions, Ollantaytambo functioned as both temple and fortress. The last stop on the Sacred Valley, it was built deep into a sheer mountainside, using massive stones to form terraces. It was also the last stop for the Incas, who were forced to retreat here after

Sacsayhuamán was sacked by the Spanish. Lying below the ruins is the village of the same name, laid out in an impressive, neat city grid.

The Sacsayhuamán fortress with electioneering graffiti carved into the hill beyond by a local politician

The Inca culture

'The Incas lived in a land of violent contrasts... In Inca Land one may pass from glaciers to tree ferns within a few hours. So also in the labyrinth of contemporary chronicles of the last of the Incas – no historians go more rapidly from fact to fancy, from accurate observation to grotesque imagination; no writers omit important details and give conflicting statements with greater frequency. The story of the Incas is still in a maze of doubt and contradiction.'

Hiram Bingham, *Explorations in the Highlands of Peru*, 1922

Inca beliefs

The centre of the Incas' empire may have been Cusco, but the spiritual home of the Incas is Lake Titicaca, where they believed they were created. Incas worshipped nature, and the three levels of existence as they perceived it are represented by the snake, symbolising the underworld; the puma, representing the earth; and the condor, emblem of the sky. Rather like the Eastern concept of yin and yang, Incas saw the world as *hanan* (male, right, superior) and *hurin* (feminine, left, inferior). The Inca

Incan agricultural techniques live on today

religion was pantheist, worshipping the sun god and the earth goddess, a practice that continues today.

Divination was key to the Incas. No important decisions were made – from diagnosing an illness to solving a crime – without consulting the Oracles. This may have involved reading the cocoa leaves 'in a teacup', or looking for signs in the carcass of a sacrificed animal. In times of great crisis or celebrations, human sacrifices would be made, sometimes on a large scale.

A strict hierarchy

The social structure of the Incas was clearly defined. While the Inca king lived in a gold palace and drank out of gold cups, the typical worker inhabited a one-room windowless mud building and slept on the floor. Inca society was based on the *ayllu* – a group of families who lived together and shared their livestock and land.

Part of the reason for the huge success of the Inca empire was the strict organisation of everything they did – from art to agriculture. The artistic approach was characterised by geometric forms and stylised representations of animals that dominated the art of other cultures. Inca architecture was superlative for its time. Without using the wheel or animals, the Incas created the incredible structures you see now.

Quechua market day

They developed almost half of the agricultural products that are eaten around the world today, including corn, potatoes, beans and peppers, which still form the basis of the Andean diet.

Alive and well

The Incas and their extraordinary empire are considered part of ancient history, wiped out by the Spanish 500 years ago, yet the Inca spirit is still very much alive. Inca culture continues to be expressed all over the Andes through the indigenous peoples that make up nearly half of Peru's populace. They continue Inca agricultural practices such as terracing and pagan celebrations such as the solstice; and, perhaps most importantly, they speak the Inca language of Quechua. Indigenous decorative arts also demonstrate this culture, as well as the wearing of headgear specific to a region, as in Inca times.

Tours and trains to Machu Picchu

There is an overwhelming choice of tours available to Machu Picchu. Rather than pick the absolutely cheapest tour for the Inca Trail, spare a thought for the hardworking guides who are often treated like mules. Even those working for decent companies are paid very little, so tip them as much as you can afford. If travelling by train, you can arrange the tickets yourself, or choose a package.

The Inca Trail

Those trekking the Inca Trail (*see p70*) must now travel as part of an organised group. Check carefully, but most tours cover the admission charge to Machu Picchu, transportation to and from the trail, an English-speaking guide, tents, mattress, three meals daily and porters to carry food and so on. If you want a porter to carry your rucksack, or a train ticket back to Cusco, it must be arranged separately and an extra fee paid. Groups are normally from 12 to 15 people; 'Premium' tours provide smaller groups and an upgrade on the train back to Cusco.

Taking the train

The four-hour train ride from Cusco travels the 115km (71 miles) to Aguas

Walking alongside Inca Trail porters

ON THE TRAIL

Make sure not only to pick up all your litter, but to look out for others littering, and, if you have space, pick up any rubbish that they may have left. Don't build any fires or pick flowers of any description en route. Trekkers need to be fully equipped with sleeping bag, tent and wet-weather gear (including boots), all of which can be rented in Cusco.

Quechua dancers greet the Hiram Bingham train

Calientes (Hot Springs), from where buses run throughout the day to take visitors up to the ruins. Trains depart from Cusco between 6am and 7am and return from between 7pm and 9pm, with a first stop at Poroy. A Vistadome ticket includes a seat with panoramic windows, drinks and snacks; the Backpacker ticket is the 'no frills' option. If you are visiting the Sacred Valley (*see p64*), it is sensible to make the train trip from Ollantaytambo, which takes only 90 minutes.

The Hiram Bingham train is the luxury option: it is extremely expensive. The three-and-a-half-hour journey begins at Poroy (20 minutes from Cusco) at a more civilised 9am and returns at 9.25pm (*Mon–Sat*). Tickets include brunch, afternoon tea and a four-course dinner with cocktails and entertainment on the way back. For full details of times and prices for any of these options, consult *www.perurail.com*

The train route

From Cusco, the train makes a series of dramatic switchbacks. At Poroy, the route traces the foothills of the Andes before descending into the lush Sacred Valley, dotted with pretty villages. The train follows the deep red waters of the Urubamba River for much of the journey, winding its way through deep gorges and past Inca fortresses. On the approach to Aguas Calientes, the landscape becomes more tropical, with exotic flowers and vegetation.

Walk: Machu Picchu – the Inca Trail

The Inca Trail is one of the most famous walks in the world. It transports trekkers through a landscape of snowcapped mountains, misty cloud forest and spectacular Inca ruins, before rewarding them with the sight of the magical 'lost city' at sunrise on the final day. Anyone of reasonable fitness can complete this walk, but you must be acclimatised before setting off.

Numbers are limited, so book ahead. Guides must be hired and porters can be arranged. The trail normally takes four days, including three nights' camping and an optional final night in Aguas Calientes. Although it is a total distance of 43km (27 miles), this includes several high passes, one of which is 4,200m (13,780ft).

Groups arrive by train, getting off at stop Kilometre 88 (88km/54½ miles from Cusco along the railway to Aguas Calientes) and walking – first on flat terrain, and then increasingly uphill – to the first site on the trail.

1 Llactapata

There are ruins of a fortress and

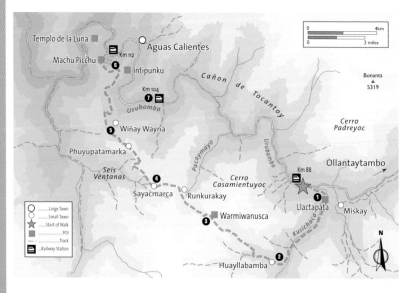

terracing here at 2,600m (8,531ft), thought to have once been a big Inca centre for agriculture.

The trail climbs steadily to the next village on the route.

2 Huayllabamba

Here, there are the remains of a stone wall from a fortress and some basic facilities in the village.

The trail climbs, offering views of the river below and glimpses of orchids and ferns. Towards the end of this section, the scenery changes dramatically from forest to grassy slopes before the path ascends even more to reach the appropriately named Warmiwanusca (Dead Woman's Pass).

3 Warmiwanusca (Dead Woman's Pass)

This is the first pass and, at 4,198m (13,774ft), the highest point on the whole trail. The views from here, if the weather is good, are spectacular.

The trail drops steeply into the Pacaymayo Valley, following a stone-laid path. It eventually arrives at the second pass (3,860m/12,664ft), with its panoramic views, and continues to descend to Sayacmarca.

4 Sayacmarca

It is possible to make out the remains of the stone walls of a fortress at this 'Inaccessible Town' (which is how the name translates).

The vegetation becomes denser on this section of the trail, which passes through cloud forest.

5 Wiñay Wayna

Houses and agricultural terracing cling to this Inca vantage point, a kind of Machu Picchu in miniature, where the 19 fountains may have been used to worship water.

Most groups leave at 5am (the trail is not open before then for safety reasons) in time to reach the entrance to Machu Picchu by dawn.

6 Intipunku (the Sun Gate)

Here, at the original entrance, walkers blink in the rising sun at the sight of Machu Picchu laid out beneath them.

From the Sun Gate, it is a 1-hour descent to Machu Picchu.

7 The mini Inca Trail

There is also a shorter version of the Inca Trail, taking only one or two days. It includes just the last section, the highlight of the whole route.

From Cusco, take the train to Aguas Calientes, getting off at Km 104 to walk up to Wiñay Wayna. Some sections here, however, are even steeper than those on the trail 'proper'.

You won't get to the site in time for a guided tour, but most people take a bus to the town of Aguas Calientes to spend the night in a hotel, before returning for sunrise and their tour next morning. You can then take a train back to Cusco in the afternoon.

Machu Picchu

Machu Picchu is a trip to the serenity of the soul, to the eternal fusion with the cosmos; where we feel our fragility. It is one of the greatest marvels of South America. A resting place of butterflies in the epicentre of the great circle of life. One more miracle.

Pablo Neruda,
The Heights of Machu Picchu

Extraordinarily, Machu Picchu was 'discovered' only in 1911, and then by accident. The American explorer Hiram Bingham stumbled across the lost city consumed by jungle while searching for the ruins of Vilcambamba. For 50 years, he maintained that it *was* Vilcambamba. Today, the Peruvian government is threatening to sue Yale University in an attempt to retrieve

The mystical city from a nearby peak

nearly 5,000 artefacts, including ceramics, cloths and metalwork that Bingham removed from the site.

The most well-known Inca site is actually the least understood. It is still not known why this city in the clouds was built at all. It was meticulously constructed, with tremendous skill and feats of labour, in the middle of the 15th century, yet it was abandoned less than 100 years later. Bingham wrongly theorised that Machu Picchu was a temple for virgin priestesses, after identifying 80 per cent of the skeletons as female. It is now known that the split was more like 50/50.

Now, it is generally agreed that the site was used as a ceremonial and, to a lesser extent, administrative and agricultural centre. Machu Picchu, whose name means 'Old Peak', was most likely a cross between a royal estate and religious retreat. The Incas viewed the landscape as integral to the architecture, so that existing stone formations were developed, not destroyed, rock was used as a sculpting block, and water sources were integrated into the buildings.

Take several hours to explore the site, making time to savour a little solitude away from the tour groups. Around 1,000 people once lived here – the majority of them priests, women and children. Their voices would have echoed through the clear mountain air to the noisy central square and up the steep walkways where llamas still roam. The houses, grouped around a communal courtyard, all had thatched roofs; livestock was kept in central enclosures, and corn was grown on the outskirts.

The **Agricultural Sector** includes remains of farm workers' houses sitting among agricultural terracing. The **Funerary Rock** is here, a large flat stone where the dead bodies were laid out to dry before being mummified.

The **Sun Temple** could be accessed only by the high priests, functioning as both solar observatory and an altar where animals were sacrificed. Underneath is the **Royal Tomb**, where nobles of the Inca aristocracy were laid to rest.

At the heart of Machu Picchu is the **Main Plaza**, where the population was addressed and ceremonies conducted. On a pyramid above the plaza is **Intiwatana**, whose name means

The Sun Temple

'Hitching Post of the Sun'. Here, during the winter solstice, the priests would literally try to harness the sun's rays.

It is a strenuous two-and-a-half-hour return trip along a very narrow trail to the top of the verdant cone of **Huayna Picchu** (Young Peak) at the northern end of the complex (*Enter: 7am–1pm. Return: by 3pm*). The reward is a bird's-eye view of the whole site.

Cusco and Machu Picchu

The thatched roofs have gone, but the stone dwellings they sheltered remain

Adventure travel around Cusco

To absorb the beauty of the Cusco area properly, and to have a well earned thrill after all that historical sightseeing, take to the water, the saddle, two wheels or even the skies. Cusco's diverse nature and rugged geography make it one of the best bases for adventure travel in the whole of South America. For rafting and flying, you will need a guide, but riding or biking can be done either as a tour or independently. Experience is

A balloon trip over Machu Picchu

not necessary for any of these activities, but a guide is advised for first-timers.

All these activities can be enjoyed as a day trip, or for longer. They do not need to be booked in advance. In fact, since unpredictable weather can influence the best places to raft or bike, it is often best to wait and make plans on arrival, taking account of local weather conditions. The dry season runs from May to October; the wet season from November to April. If necessary, wet-weather gear, and hard hats, can be purchased or hired from local outfitters.

With your own group (which can be as small as two people), it is possible to tailor your trip to suit both your interests and your schedule. So, for example, a rafting trip in the Sacred Valley can be combined with a trip to Pisac market or to the ruins at Ollantaytambo nearby.

Horse-riding

Horses can be hired to visit almost any part of the Sacred Valley, but a particularly good tour is the half-day trip from Cusco to Sacsayhuamán. After visiting this impressive Inca site, the horses are ridden to a moon temple and natural caves, and then on to the archaeological ruins at Tambomachay and Pucapucara, with transfers back to Cusco.

Mountain biking

The area's huge mountains and deep valleys offer a roller-coaster ride for cyclists. Mountain bikes can be hired in Cusco, but do thorough safety checks (particularly on the brakes), and be prepared for unpaved roads and erratic traffic. For those seeking something altogether more sedate, a gentle pedal along the valley floor on a one-day trip in the Sacred Valley may appeal.

Paragliding and hot-air ballooning

The Sacred Valley, with its good thermals and even better scenery, is the place to soar in the sky, either as a paraglider or in a colourful hot-air balloon. Flights normally take place in the morning and may hover over the Sacsayhuamán Inca ruins or even over the great citadel of Machu Picchu itself for the ultimate 'trip'.

Rafting

The Urubamba River, which flows down from the Andes and through the heart of the scenic Sacred Valley, offers good, though gentle, rafting (Class I and II). For those with experience who really want to shoot the rapids, the Apurímac River (Class III and IV), four hours from Cusco, is one of the top ten places to go rafting in the world. Trips offered to Apurímac are normally for four days (see p147).

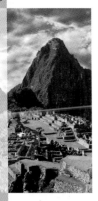

Excursion: Train to Lake Titicaca

One of the highest train journeys in the world runs south from Cusco to Puno on the northern shores of Lake Titicaca. The route goes through the Sacred Valley, across undulating plains and past snow-capped mountains. It gives a taste of local life, with a glass observation carriage that allows travellers to enjoy the scenery. The 388km (241-mile) journey can also be made by bus or by plane, and can be done in reverse.

The train

Trains depart from Cusco at 8am on Mondays, Wednesdays and Saturdays, arriving at 6pm in Puno. They leave from Wanchaq station – which is different from the station for Machu Picchu. Make reservations at least one day in advance – either at the station or through any of the travel agents in Cusco. First-class tickets are six times the price of Backpacker class, which can be rather uncomfortable. The extra

A boat on Lake Titicaca, made from tortura reeds

The train stops again at the halfway point of El Paso de la Raya, which, at 4,319m (14,171ft), is the highest point on the route and a chilly, deserted spot. The train also makes a number of other, shorter stops en route, where children and women hawk food and handicrafts – particularly clothing and toys made from guinea-pig fur. After 280km (174 miles), at around 4.30pm, the train arrives at Juliaca, where it stops for another buying opportunity, before finally pulling in to Puno.

Puno

The city's full name is San Carlos de Puno, founded in 1668 when silver was discovered nearby. At 3,800m (12,468ft) in the middle of the rather bleak *altiplano* (high plateau), Puno can get very cold, so consider visiting the central market for a warm alpaca jumper and maybe some souvenirs. Puno is a workaday city, with just a small cluster of historical buildings, and is mainly used as a jumping-off point for Lake Titicaca. However, it does boast the title of 'folkloric capital of Peru' because of its many local dances and festivals. On the Plaza de Armas, the cathedral (1757) is grand rather than lustrous, with a battered Baroque façade and rather plain interior. Uphill three blocks is Huajsapata Park, with an enormous white statue of Manco Cápac, said to have been the first Inca. He looks over the city towards Lake Titicaca, the place of his birth, apparently enjoying the view.

Puno, on the edge of Lake Titicaca

cash also buys you a three-course lunch. For the latest information, visit the PeruRail website *www.perurail.com*

The journey

The train makes a gentle climb out of Cusco, travelling alongside the winding Huatanay River. After 40km (25 miles), it passes the stone gate of Rumicolca that once guarded Cusco. A few kilometres on is the splendid colonial church at Andahuaylillas, then Lake Urcos, and then a series of small villages come into view. At nearly the third-way mark, on the approach to San Pedro station, look out for Viracocha, the temple dedicated to the creator god. There is a scheduled stop at Sicuani, a chance to buy snacks and even souvenirs.

Arequipa and the Colca Canyon

Peru's second city is also one of its most elegant. Wide avenues on a rectangular grid surround the centrepiece, Plaza de Armas, a lush and calming square lined with colonnades and overlooked by the city's cathedral. In fact, the cathedral is one of many religious gems here, the best of which is perhaps the Monasterio de Santa Catalina, a sprawling convent with a fascinating and scandalous past.

Beyond the city limits, things are no less interesting. The two deepest canyons in the world are in this region, and then there are the surrounding volcanoes that have played their part in Arequipa's history. The city was destroyed in 1600, and earthquakes have recurred over the centuries, but Arequipeños are proud of their volcanoes, particularly the graceful El Misti (5,822m/19,101ft). Its bright white volcanic rock, *sillar*, has lent its dazzling looks to many of the city's buildings.

The mountainous peaks are popular with climbers too, and have yielded several important archaeological finds, including the body of an Inca girl sacrificed on a mountain top and preserved in ice for 500 years. To the west of the city lies Toro Muerto, a volcanic desert strewn with boulders, hundreds of which have had images carved upon them by ancient cultures.

Arequipa is just over 1,000km (621 miles) south of Lima, and flights from the capital take around one hour. Travel by bus, along the coastal Pan-American Highway, is somewhat slower and can take up to 16 hours, depending on the company and route.

AREQUIPA'S HISTORIC CENTRE

The city gets an average of 300 sunny days a year, the nights are pleasant, and the altitude of 2,400m (7,874ft) makes it a good place to acclimatise before heading to Cusco, or even higher. The historic centre of the city, known as

THE WHITE CITY

There are two schools of thought on why Arequipa is nicknamed the Ciudad Blanca (White City). Some believe it is to do with the white volcanic stone thrown up by the volcanoes that overlook the city, and from which many of the colonial buildings were constructed. The other theory (and no one knows for sure which is correct) is that the name was given by Peruvian natives in colonial times when more Spanish lived in Arequipa than anywhere else on the South American continent.

El Cercado (The Surrounded One), is now a UNESCO World Heritage Site. Colourfully painted colonial mansions, impressive churches and a thriving cultural scene await the visitor.

Casa Arróspide (Casa Iriberry)

On the corner of San Agustín and Santa Catalina, this mansion is home to the Cultural Centre of San Agustín University. It hosts temporary photographic exhibitions and changing displays of contemporary art. The art shop is also worth a look, and the terrace café has fine views over the cathedral.

Santa Catalina 101. Tel: (054) 204 482. Mon–Sat 10am–6pm. Free admission.

La Casa de Tristán del Pozo

The large arched portal of this 1730s mansion is intricately decorated with religious motifs. Once a seminary, the building is now

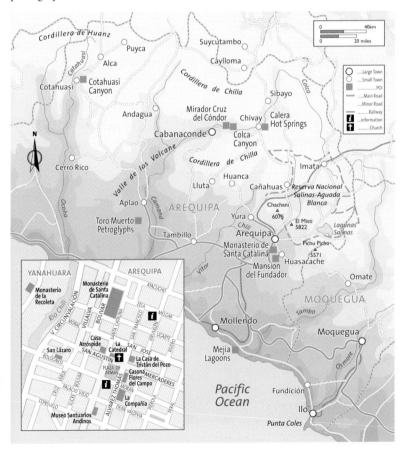

a bank, but you can wander into the spacious interior courtyard with its fearsome gargoyles, and there is also a small museum within.
San Francisco 108. Open: Mon–Sat 9am–noon & 4–7pm. Free admission.

Casona Flores del Campo

On the east side of the Plaza de Armas, this is one of the oldest houses in Arequipa, though it took 200 years to complete. It suffers from a lack of funds and the effects of successive earthquakes, but there are still some interesting period features on view – particularly the old beams still held together by llama-skin ties!

Portal de Flores 136. Tel: (054) 244 150. Open: 10am–5pm. Free admission.

Museo Santuarios Andinos

This small museum's most famous attraction is the frozen body of 'Juanita', the young Inca girl who was discovered in near perfect condition on top of the Ampato volcano in 1995. She was killed as a sacrificial offering to the mountain gods and buried in a tomb with a number of funeral offerings that are also on display in the museum. She is joined here by other mummies found on the mountain. Juanita had been preserved in ice for hundreds of years, and was found after an eruption propelled her from her

Arequipa's elegant central square

The mummified remains of the Ice Princess in Museo Santuarios Andinos

grave. The 'Ice Princess' is displayed in a refrigerated glass case, and the museum tour includes a video documenting the discovery.

Santa Catalina 210. Tel: (054) 200 345. Open: Mon–Sat 9am–6pm, Sun 9am–3pm. Admission charge.

Plaza de Armas

Almost every South American city has one, but the main square in Arequipa is something special. While you plan your tour of the city, rest up in one of the bars overlooking the plaza and appreciate the tall palms, lush planting and elaborate fountain that stands in the centre.

RELIGIOUS RICHES

The area around Arequipa had been inhabited for over 6,000 years before the city was 'founded' by Garcí Manuel de Carbajal on 15 August 1540. As a major trading post, it was not long before the town was filled with wealthy and pious Spanish, intent on demonstrating their love of God through spectacular religious buildings, notably the cathedral and the Santa Catalina convent.

La Catedral

Spanning the whole north side of the main plaza is the glittering *sillar* façade of Arequipa's cathedral. Almost from the day it was commissioned in 1544, the construction was plagued by earthquakes and eruptions, and in 1844 a huge fire caused major damage. In 1868, the towers were rebuilt by a local architect in the neoclassical style, and so the cathedral today is a mix of styles from the 17th and 18th centuries. In 2001, another earthquake damaged one of the towers, but this has since been restored. Inside, the cathedral is adorned with Carrara marble and wood, the pulpit is neo-Gothic French

A FUN CONVENT

In colonial times, it was traditional for the second daughter of wealthy families to dedicate her life to God. Compared to most convents, Santa Catalina's design was spacious and well appointed. Before long, rich young women were moving in with their fine dresses, linens, paintings, servants and slaves, not to mention the musicians who were regularly brought in to play at parties. The fun and games continued until 1871, when the pope appointed Sister Josefa Cadena to reform the convent. The servants and slaves were released, and life in the convent under the strict Dominican nun became much less attractive for Arequipa's social butterflies. Most left, although many of their servants and slaves stayed on to become nuns.

The intricately carved cloisters of La Compañia Jesuit complex date from the 17th century

and the massive 19th-century pipe organ was built by Loret of Belgium. *Plaza de Armas. Free admission.*

La Compañía

Opposite the cathedral is the Baroque entrance to an atmospheric Jesuit church completed in 1698 and largely untouched by the earthquakes that have played havoc with Arequipa. Inside, the main altar is carved from cedar and covered in gold. On the flanks are two chapels, the Capilla Real and Capilla de San Ignacio, the latter of which is adorned with colourful images. Next to the church, with their intricate carved arches and gargoyles, are the cloisters that were once part of the Jesuits' complex but now house shops and offices. *Plaza de Armas. Admission charge for Capilla de San Ignacio.*

Cloister of the Orange Trees, Santa Catalina

Monasterio de Santa Catalina

A true masterpiece of colonial architecture, this convent is a large complex of rooms, picturesque plazas, ornate fountains and a maze of narrow, cobblestone streets. Construction began in 1579 and went on for decades, but, at its completion, it was practically a town within the town, covering an area of 20,000sq m (215,200sq ft), with space for 450 nuns to live in 'seclusion' (*see box opposite*). The convent finally opened its doors to the public in 1970, and a walk through its cloisters and cobbled streets is a peaceful delight.

Santa Catalina 301. Tel: (054) 229 798. www.santacatalina.org.pe. Open: 9am–5pm. Last entrance: 4pm. Admission charge.

A narrow street in San Lázaro

AREQUIPA'S NEIGHBOURHOODS

Attractive as the stylish centre of
Arequipa is, there are plenty of reasons
to venture further afield. To the north is
the city's oldest neighbourhood of San
Lázaro, with its chapel and narrow
streets. Across the Río Chili are the
attractive colonial suburbs of Yanahura
and Cayma, as well as the fascinating
Recoleta convent. All of these are worth
a visit, and can be reached on foot, but
some travellers prefer to take a *collectivo*
(minibus) or taxi, due to the nuisance
of street beggars (*see box*).

LIFE ON THE STREETS

Arequipa's pleasant climate has always
attracted Peru's elite, but not everyone in the
city is so well heeled. As in other Peruvian
cities, street beggars are common here, but
they seem more incongruous in these elegant
surroundings. It is best not to give money to
them, as it encourages more begging and
more persistent tactics. Occasionally, tourists
have reported incidences of muggings;
visitors should not be paranoid, but take
sensible precautions and don't go out on long
walks alone.

Cayma

Located 3km (1³/4 miles) from the
centre, past Yanahura, is this semi-
agricultural district, with its
picturesque terraced farms that supply
the markets of Arequipa. There are
some good views over the city, and in
the main plaza is a 200-year-old church
housing the image of the Virgin of the
Candlemas, which was donated by King
Carlos V of Spain.
*Iglesia San Miguel, Cayma. Open:
9am–4pm. Free admission to church.*

San Lázaro

The first Spanish settlers in Arequipa
gravitated to San Lázaro, a pretty
district full of narrow, winding streets.
The church in this small
neighbourhood is the oldest in
Arequipa and was originally built as a
Dominican hermitage.
*Iglesia San Lázaro, Avenida Juan
de la Torre, Barrio de San Lázaro.
Open: irregular hours.
Free admission to church.*

Yanahuara

Originally a native village 2km
(1¼ miles) from the centre, Yanahuara
has been swallowed up by the
expanding city. It remains a maze of
narrow, colourful alleys, and charming
houses with private orchards. The
mestizo (mixed race) church in the
main square here dates from 1750, and,
though the interior is relatively modest,
the façade is fine Baroque. The vantage
point of the arched Mirador, with its
engraved *sillar* arches, provides
spectacular views of the city and the
three volcanoes that watch over it.
Free admission to church.

Monasterio de la Recoleta

Across the Río Chili, in Yanahura, is
a Franciscan convent founded in 1648,
with cloisters that exemplify Arequipa's
colonial architecture. Although the
original buildings were destroyed by
earthquakes, the library houses over
25,000 precious works, with many more
than 500 years old. At the back of the
convent is a collection of specimens
and artefacts gathered by the
missionaries on their trips into the
Amazon jungle.
*Jirón Recoleta 117. Tel: (054) 270 966.
Open: Mon–Sat 9am–noon & 2–5.30pm.
Admission charge.*

Yanahuara's arched *Mirador*, with snow-capped El Misti rising beyond the city

AROUND AREQUIPA

The countryside around Arequipa is some of the most spectacular and varied in Peru, and is also the source of the exquisitely fine alpaca wool that is one of the region's principal exports. From the city centre, the attractions listed here can be visited on organised tours, or the more independently minded can make their own way by bus, hire car or taxi.

Canyons

A visit to the Colca Canyon (*see p88*) affords jaw-dropping views and the chance to get close to the Andean condor. Only one canyon in the whole world is deeper than the Colca; this too is in the region of Arequipa and is named the Cotahuasi (*see p122*).

Lagoons and birdwatching

Lagunas Salinas, beyond El Misti (*see opposite*), is a salt lake famed for its birding opportunities. If the rainy season is too dry, the flamingoes may not show, but you are still likely to see crested ducks, Andean geese and Aplomado falcons. On the coast, 100km (62 miles) south of the city, are the Mejía Lagoons, with the chance to spot over 150 species, including the tricoloured heron and red-fronted coot. Both the Salinas and Mejía are designated as national sanctuaries.

Mansión del Fundador (Mansion of the Founder)

Restored to its former glory in the 1980s, the home of Garcí Manuel de Carbajal, who founded Arequipa on

Lush countryside with El Misti and his brothers in the background

Francisco Pizarro's orders, sits next to the Socabaya River in Huasacache, 20km (12½ miles) southeast of the centre. The mansion was restored in 1821 with period paintings and furniture, and its gardens are a delight. The flat road from Arequipa passes through some scenic countryside, so a half-day mountain-bike tour is a popular and environmentally friendly option. Tours by bike or minibus can be booked at any of the agencies on the street named Jerusalén in Arequipa, and generally take in the 17th-century water-powered mill at Sabandía.
Villa Paisajista, Huasacache. Tel: (054) 225 200. Mansion and mill open: 9am–5pm. Admission charge.

El Misti

Standing proudly between his two brothers Chachani (6,075m/19,932ft) and Pichu Pichu (5,571m/18,278ft), El Misti (The Gentleman) (5,822m/19,102ft) is the emblematic mountain of Arequipa. Experienced guides can take you on an overnight hike to the top, provided you are fit. A four-wheel drive will drop you as high as possible (about 3,300m/10,827ft), and, after the five-hour hike, camp is made at around 4,500m (14,765ft). The next day, a six-hour hike brings you almost to the summit, where the views are breathtaking. The more experienced can carry on another couple of hundred metres to the very top, but crampons and ice axes will be required.

Petroglyphs at Toro Muerto

Toro Muerto petroglyphs

This barren desert 150km (93 miles) west of the city is home to the famous petroglyphs, one of Arequipa's most intriguing attractions. On hundreds of boulders scattered around the landscape visitors can see intricate etchings of snakes, birds, feline creatures and all manner of mysterious shapes. It's thought that the Wari culture began the tradition over 1,000 years ago, and subsequent cultures continued it, but no evidence of human occupancy has been found to confirm the theories. Organised overnight trips can be arranged from the city.

Excursion: Colca Canyon

As spectacular as the Grand Canyon, and twice as deep, the Colca is also a living canyon populated by farmers, and covered in Inca-style terraces that provide food for the people who live here. This is also one of the few places where you can see the Andean condor up close in flight.

Visitors with plenty of time can opt for a three- or four-day trek down into the canyon, but the popular two-day tour described here is enough to give a flavour of the place.

Tour buses can be crowded in high season (*July & Aug*), which in the heat at high altitude can be unpleasant. If your budget will stretch to it, hire a guide with a private four-wheel drive.

Day 1
On the way to the canyon
Leave Arequipa around 8am, or earlier if you plan to trek into the canyon from Cabanaconde. On the way to the canyon, you may encounter llamas and their smaller cousins, alpacas and vicuñas, in the *altiplano* (highland) countryside. Stop for lunch in the small town of Chivay (3,500m/11,484ft), and acclimatise with a postprandial stroll.

HEAD TO THE MARKET

Meals are not included in the price of most tours, and the chosen restaurant stops are often overpriced and below par. Detour to Chivay's great market to find your own lunch – you'll save money and have a more enjoyable experience.

View from the Mirador, Colca Canyon

Calera Hot Springs, overnight in Chivay
Even a short hike at this altitude can be strenuous, so it's wise to take it easy on the first day. The Calera Hot Springs at Chivay are some of the best in South America, and the three pools of different temperatures will help to soothe your aches away.
Calera Hot Springs, Chivay. Open: 10am–5pm. Admission charge.

Day 2
Mirador Cruz del Cóndor,
return to Arequipa

Perched on the edge of the canyon is this frighteningly high lookout, a 90-minute drive from Chivay followed by a breathless 40-minute hike. Buses leave Chivay early, as the condors are less active in the afternoon. Few people ever get close to condors in flight: at 15kg (33lb), with a wingspan of 3.5m (11ft), they need strong thermals to take off and fly, and are usually too far up for a proper look. Here, though, they soar around within metres of the Mirador, often so close you can hear them twist their wings. It's easy to see why the Incas thought the condor, up close in all its majesty, was a divine messenger.

The view from the lookout is a dizzying sight, with the canyon dropping 1,200m (3,937ft) to the valley floor below, and the mountains towering into the sky above. What adds to the thrilling sensation is that there are no railings here – don't get too close to the edge. The agricultural terraces spread out below are tended cooperatively by groups of families, and are irrigated by melting snow from the peaks above, just as they were in the days of the Incas.

The two-day tour gets back to Arequipa at about 5pm. Hikers travelling on to Cabanaconde should visit *www.hoteltintin.com/colcaing.php* for details of extended treks into the canyon.

Excursion: Colca Canyon

Bountiful produce in Chivay's market

Lake Titicaca

According to legend, Manco Cápac and his sister consort Mama Ocllo left their father the Sun and came down to earth. Here, they rose from the depths of Lake Titicaca and were sent by the Sun to found Cusco. In Inca mythology, this sacred lake is the equivalent of the Garden of Eden. Almost 15 times as large as Lake Geneva, the expansive mass is a dazzling mirror of the blue sky above. When viewed from the highest point on one of its peaceful islands, the serenity and beauty of the scene are breathtaking.

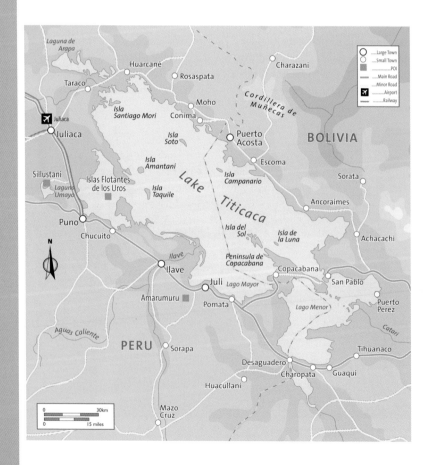

Lake Titicaca is the spiritual home of the Incas

Most visitors to the area arrive in Puno via the city of Juliaca, one of Peru's busiest road and rail junctions, with the airport nearest to the lake. From Puno, visitors can explore the lake by boat on one of the many excursions organised by the entrepreneurial locals. Most visitors need to acclimatise before travelling to the Lake Titicaca area, so try to spend time lower down first, perhaps in Cusco or Arequipa. At an altitude of over 3,800m (12,468ft), just walking around can exhaust even a fit person, and altitude sickness is common.

Tours of the unique floating reed islands near Puno take only a few hours, or visitors can travel further onto the lake and spend a few days appreciating the traditional way of life on the islands of Taquile and Amantaní. Further south, lying within the Bolivian part of the lake, is Isla del Sol (Island of the Sun), the legendary birthplace of the first Inca and the largest island on Titicaca. The neighbouring island is called Isla de la Luna (Island of the Moon) and was home to Inca priestesses.

Around the lake, there is plenty to attract the visitor, from the ancient necropolis of Sillustani with its towering mausoleums to the pleasant and relaxed colonial towns near the border with Bolivia. And, should you feel the need to let your hair down, Puno has a good selection of bars and restaurants where the local musicians earn their keep by providing entertainment.

Heaven and earth: lake and *altiplano*

If Lake Titicaca reflects the heavenly sky above, the harsh *altiplano* (highland) that borders it is unquestionably earth, and lots of it. It is a harsh homeland for the indigenous Aymara Indians who herd llama and alpaca at close to 4km (2½ miles) above sea level, and tend their meagre crops in biting winds and burning sun. Yet it is also a beautiful landscape, dotted with friendly and lively towns, and small communities where people live a forgotten way of life, cooperating with each other for the common good.

A Colla tomb at Sillustani

THE PLIGHT OF THE AYMARA

The town of Ilave, 55km (34 miles) south of Puno, is notorious as the place where a crowd of angry Aymara Indians lynched their mayor in 2004 after he ignored weeks of anti-corruption protests. Once subjects of the Spanish and before that the Incas, these indigenous people are still at the bottom of the pile, and have benefited little from Peru's recent economic success. For visitors, being charged admission to churches, having to tip for photographs, and the general hard-sell, particularly around Puno, can sometimes be annoying, but bear in mind that a small donation might well go towards schoolbooks for Aymara children.

Lake Titicaca

Only one river flows out of Lake Titicaca, taking with it just 5 per cent of the water that two dozen other rivers feed into the lake. The remaining influx evaporates under the harsh sun, keeping the lake at a more or less steady level.

Titicaca is home to a giant frog that was discovered by Jacques Cousteau in 1973. He was looking for sunken Inca treasure, but found these 26cm (10in) long amphibians instead – hidden in the depths, away from the ultraviolet solar radiation that could kill them. Catfish and killifish are also found, a rare source of protein in the local diet. The best views of the lake are from its islands, so visitors are encouraged to join an excursion (*see p96*).

Puno

Capital of a large region that stretches from the Amazon basin in the north almost to the border with Chile, this once silver-rich city still has some buildings of note (*see p77*), but its big draw is the boat excursions that leave from here to explore the lake (*see p96*). It also has a reputation as something of a party town, and there always seems to be a festival of some sort going on.

Sillustani

This ancient burial site near Puno is unusual for its well-preserved circular towers in which the dead were entombed. These towers are several metres tall; many of them were built by the Collas, an Aymara tribe that was conquered by the Incas, but a range of styles can be seen, suggesting that they were constructed at different periods. It is possible that the Pukará, Tiahuanaca and even the Incas themselves built some of them.

The site is near Laguna Umayo, 15km (9½ miles) north of Puno along the main road, then another 10km (6 miles) along a side road.

An Aymara woman with her alpaca on the harsh *altiplano*

Islands in time

The floating islands of Uros on Lake Titicaca, near Puno

Surrounded on all sides by the shimmering waters of Lake Titicaca, hardy natives live simple lives of farming, fishing and textile weaving on the remote islands of Taquile and Amantaní. Closer to shore are the famous *islas flotantes* (floating islands), whose people fight a never-ending battle to stop their habitat from sinking.

Sinking fast, the floating islands

From Puno's shoreline, the floating islands resemble giant bird's nests that have fallen into the water. They are home to the Uros people, who have lived this unusual existence since Inca times. The scores of small islands that make up the community are constructed from the plentiful totora reeds that grow in Titicaca's shallow waters. The islands, 6km (3¾ miles) from Puno, are kept afloat by their hard-working inhabitants who must interweave new layers of reeds above the old on an almost daily basis.

The traditional Uros way of life revolves around fishing, and trade with mainlanders for dietary staples and cloth. The people build basic lightweight huts and fishing boats, again both from totora. Without running water and electricity, and with the constant battle to keep the waters of the lake at bay, it is a hard life. The 'ground' is prone to 'potholes', and over the years a number of children have fallen in and died, from either exposure or drowning.

The natives now have much more contact with the outside world. Previously, when a young couple married, they would traditionally build themselves a hut on a spare piece of island or, if space was limited, they would harvest some totora and create somewhere to build on. Increased tourism has all but brought an end to this way of life. Locals rely heavily on selling handicrafts to day-trippers, and charging for photographs and island tours. Many Uros people now live on the mainland, and come to the islands purely for work. Coming here can feel a little like visiting a human zoo, but tourist funds do keep the islands' small school going.

Taquile and Amantaní: the simple life

Isla Taquile, 35km (22 miles) and 2½ hours from Puno, could not be more different from the floating islands. It is not man-made and the 1,200 locals here are much more self-sufficient – not surprising since they have land on which they can grow crops. The island is 6km (3¾ miles) by 1km (½ mile), its steep western slopes covered in terraces of potatoes and quinoa (a protein-rich grain). From the boat dock, a 500-step staircase leads to the top – an exhausting climb at this altitude. A visit here feels relaxed and educational – locals can pick you up from Puno, and take you to the island for an overnight stay in a family house, where you can try your hand at blanket-weaving, herding sheep or tending the crops.

Isla Amantaní, two hours north of Taquile, is even quieter than its smaller neighbour, and is less visited. The twin peaks of Pachamama and Pachatata (Mother Earth and Father Earth), with their pre-Inca ruins, watch over the well-tended communal farms below, where natives subsist on what they can grow or catch, supplementing their income with fine textiles from sheep and alpaca wool.

Arts and crafts for sale on Uros

Excursion: Boat trips on Lake Titicaca

On the western shore of the lake is Puno's flotilla of small but generally seaworthy boats. For a reasonable charge, the locals will ferry you onto the lake for a scenic birding tour or to visit inhabited islands (see p94). Another option is to head south by land to the peninsula of Copacabana, across the border with Bolivia, and take a tour from there to the ancient Inca islands of the Sun and Moon (see p98).

Birding tours

Over 60 species of birds, both residents and migrants, can be spotted in and around the lake. Among the residents are the Andean duck, with its white beak and red plumage, and the Andean flicker, whose dried meat is a pre-Columbian treatment still eaten to increase the supply of milk in nursing women and domestic animals. Birding tours with experienced English-speaking guides can be booked at the Hotel Libertador in Puno (*Isla Esteves, Lago Titicaca. Tel: (051) 367 780. Fax: (051) 367 879*), although you may prefer to take your chances at the dock and negotiate a cheaper deal.

Island-life tour

One of the most popular tours leaves from Puno early in the morning (around 8am), arriving at the Uros *islas flotantes* (floating islands) half an hour later. Built entirely of the local totora reeds, the Uros are a truly odd phenomenon (*see p94*). On your first

stop of the day, there will be plenty of opportunities to buy all sorts of mementoes, from miniature reed boats to stuffed ducks and (usually inferior) textiles. Don't spend too much, as there are better things to buy further on.

A boy with his vicuñas, Taquile

Isla del Sol is the birthplace of the first Incas, who were sent down from the sun

The next stop is on the island of Taquile (*see p95*), another two hours into the lake. You can choose to spend a few hours on this charming and restful island, and take in lunch, before returning to Puno in time for dinner.

For a longer excursion, stay one or two nights on Taquile, or head north for another two hours to Amantaní (*see p95*), a larger island that rewards the extra investment of time with an even more relaxing experience.

Tours from Copacabana

The famous Isla del Sol (Island of the Sun) and Isla de la Luna (Island of the Moon) (*see p98*) are too far away for Puno's rickety fleet, so visitors must take a three-hour bus journey down the coast to Copacabana, which is on the Bolivian part of the lake. From here, a catamaran whisks visitors on a 30-minute ride to Isla del Sol, birthplace of the Incas, and, after an hour or two on the island, it's back to Copacabana.

Alternatively, you can take your time travelling to Copacabana, allowing you to appreciate the route down the coast. When you arrive in Copacabana, take your pick from the ferries on offer, and spend as long as you want enjoying these Inca treasure islands. Isla del Sol is a large island with Inca ruins scattered all around, and there are scenic trails with great views of the lakes. After visiting Isla de la Luna, spend the night in Copacabana itself, one of Bolivia's most important sites of pilgrimage.

Rock formations between Ilave and Juli, south of Puno

South of Puno

The road south of Puno follows Lake
Titicaca's shoreline, sometimes
swerving inland, as it meanders towards
the Bolivian border. Along the way are
many interesting villages and towns,
and spectacular viewpoints of the
southern lake. The road crosses into
Bolivia to the Copacabana Peninsula,
from where boat trips take visitors to
the islands of the Sun and Moon –
birthplace of the Incas and where the
Inca legend begins.

Amarumuru

Between Ilave and Juli, a number of
unusual rock formations rise from the
plains, including one, Amarumuru, that
resembles a massive doorway. In
Aymara legend, Amarumuru was
carved by a race of giants and is a
portal to another dimension.

Chucuito

On the southern shores of Lake
Titicaca, 18km (11 miles) from Puno,
is the picturesque town of Chucuito.
Life moves slowly here, and it's a good
place to get away from it all and
perhaps spend the night. Two churches
of note are here: Nuestra Señora de la
Asunción boasts an elaborate 400-year-
old Renaissance façade, and Iglesia
Santo Domingo can be recognised by
its ancient stone tower.
*Opening times of the churches vary.
Admission charge.*

Isla del Sol and Isla de la Luna
(Islands of the Sun and Moon)

These two islands actually lie across the
border, and can be reached by boat
excursions from the Bolivian town of
Copacabana, about 30km (18½ miles)
from Pomata. On Isla de la Luna, Inca

priestesses lived in isolation within the palace walls conducting ceremonies of worship to Inca gods. On Isla del Sol, the ruins of a temple mark the spot where the founders of the Inca dynasty, Manco Cápac and Mama Ocllo, were sent down to earth by the sun. Brother and sister, they rose from the lake to this spot, before leaving for Cusco to build their empire in the north.

Juli

Home to four beautiful colonial churches in close proximity to each other, Juli, 82km (51 miles) from Puno, was once the capital of the lake area.

The Temple of Fertility at Chucuito

EL TEMPLO DE FERTILIDAD (TEMPLE OF FERTILITY)

Next to Santo Domingo in Chucuito is a walled field, full of phallic stone sculptures pointing skywards. For years, local guides would explain to rapt tourists how maidens once visited the enclosure as part of an ancient ritual. In fact, enterprising locals moved the stones to this site only in 1993, and no one as yet knows their true origin or meaning. The stunt has certainly helped the local economy, and the 'temple' has found its way into many guides and maps.

The Spanish needed one church for themselves, one for *mestizo* (mixed race) Christians, and the other two for all the natives they planned to convert. From the courtyard of La Asunción, visitors have a great view of the lake, while the Jesuit church of Santa Cruz is notable for its façade featuring the Inca sun god, carved by native stonemasons. *Churches open: 9am–noon. Admission charge.*

Pomata

The Iglesia Santiago Apóstol is a 17th-century church, 23km (14 miles) from Juli, with an impressive pink-granite façade, combining Spanish Christian motifs with those of the native Indians who carved it. The other church here, dating from the 18th century, features a similarly elaborate exterior with delicate alabaster windows that cast a spiritual glow over the gold-leaf-covered altar. *Opening times of churches vary. Admission charge.*

The Amazon

At the mention of the Amazon, most people will think of Brazil, but in fact the mighty river has its source in the Peruvian Andes. By far the most biodiverse region on earth, the importance of the Amazon cannot be overstated – without it to regulate our climate there would be global devastation. By coming to this area with a responsible tour agency, and taking care not to damage its precious ecosystems, visitors can help to preserve this wonder – and the world – for future generations.

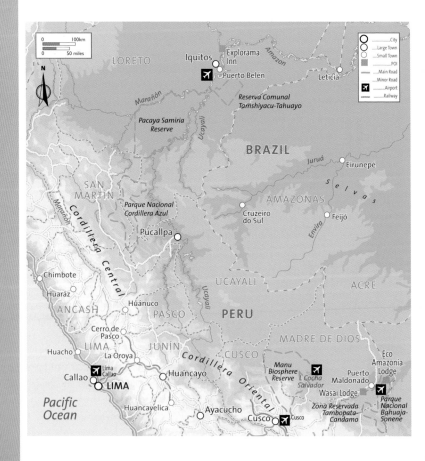

Essentially, there are two routes into Peru's Amazon basin. Visitors can fly from Lima into the time-trapped jungle town of Iquitos in the country's northern Amazon, or choose to head south into the vast jungle near Puerto Maldonado – a half-hour flight from Cusco and two hours from Lima. There are no roads to Iquitos, and the roads to Puerto Maldonado are little more than bumpy dirt tracks, for masochists only.

In the north, elegant flat-bottom river boats can transport you in luxury from Iquitos deep into the Pacaya Samiria Reserve to see pink dolphins, angry caimans and careless monkeys, while inexpensive jungle lodges offer the chance to explore the forest at close quarters, on the ground or up in the canopy.

The treasures of the southern jungle are no less impressive, with national parks the size of countries containing countless species of birds, plants, insects and mammals. The Manu Biosphere Reserve covers a huge, sparsely populated region that requires a significant investment in time and resources to visit, but true nature-lovers will be rewarded with teeming trails through pristine virgin forest, and huge spectacular lakes such as the Cocha Salvador.

More easily accessible from Puerto Maldonado are the adjacent reserves of Bahuaja-Sonene and Tambopata-Candamo. The latter in particular is well served by inexpensive jungle lodges, and is the best way to see the rainforest if your budget is limited or time is short.

The vast expanse of the Amazon river and jungle

IQUITOS AND THE NORTHERN AMAZON

Iquitos is the sort of city that should exist only in the movies – surrounded by the Amazon, isolated yet bustling with frontier characters, and dripping in atmosphere. Its population is a mix of indigenous tribes and European and Chinese immigrants, a legacy of the rubber boom that lasted from 1880 to World War I. Interesting in itself, as well as the perfect starting point for river and jungle excursions, Iquitos is 75 minutes by plane from Lima.

Iquitos

A number of buildings constructed during the rubber era are still standing in the city, including the Iron House in the main square, which was designed by Gustave Eiffel and shipped all the way from France. Along the Malecón Tarapaca, on the banks of the Amazon, there are some fine colonial mansions decorated with ceramic tiles from Portugal and Italy. North of the main square, the Malecón turns into El Boulevard – hub of the city's thriving nightlife.

Beaches, swimming and watersports

If you have some time to kill in Iquitos, there is a decent beach at Playa Nanay, 2km (1¼ miles) north of the centre – a lively spot with weekend bars and restaurants, but check with locals to make sure the swimming is safe when you are there. To the west of the centre, Lake Moronacocha is where locals go swimming and waterskiing. However, before you pull on skis, consider the disruption to local ecosystems caused

Jungle lodges around Iquitos offer a close-up view of the rainforest

From the dock in Iquitos, river boats of all shapes and sizes head along the Amazon

by watersports, not to mention the environmental cost of getting fuel to this remote jungle outpost.

Exploring the jungle

From Iquitos, the easiest, most comfortable and most expensive way to see the jungle is on one of the plush river boats that are best booked before you leave home (*see p104*). You can get to Iquitos and wait for a boat that suits you, but you may find the more well-appointed vessels fully booked by US tour groups. One benefit of these river cruises is that you can travel much further into the interior, reaching parts of the Pacaya Samiria Reserve, for example, that are very rarely visited (*see p104*).

A more rustic option is to head for one of the many jungle lodges in the region. There are many to choose from (*see p171*) with varying levels of comfort to suit different pockets. Individual lodges offer their own activities, but staples are guided hikes beneath the canopy, motor-canoe day trips and night excursions on the river, birdwatching and fishing – sometimes for piranha.

Puerto Belén

Before you leave for the jungle, you will probably stock up at the market in Puerto Belén. The houses in this quarter, a few blocks south of the centre, are built on stilts or rafts to accommodate the Amazon's high-water season. With its bare-bones shanty-town vibe, Belén has changed little since the rubber boom, and was featured in Werner Herzog's epic film *Fitzcarraldo*. The crowded market is a pickpocket's paradise, so be careful.

Excursion: Sail through the jungle

One of the most comfortable ways to explore the Amazon is with a river cruise from Iquitos. Take care when booking – some boats have deep draughts that harm river life, and older vessels leak oil. Look for statements about sustainable tourism on company websites, and if possible choose to travel with a member of the International Ecotourism Society (see www.ecotourism.org for a list of members).

Day 1
From Iquitos into the past
After breakfast, take a stroll around the city (*see p102*), then step aboard. For a

A spider monkey spots the river boat

truly evocative experience, book a cabin on one of the 19th-century-style flat-bottom river boats, travelling into the remote Pacaya Samiria Reserve. These are luxury cruises of at least five days, but the ever-changing scenery and wildlife more than make up for the outlay, and boredom will not be a problem. As the deckhands weigh anchor, enjoy an alfresco lunch and get used to life on the river. Later, get to know your shipmates under the vibrant night sky.

Day 2
The source of the Amazon
The boat reaches the junction of the Ucayali and Marañón rivers, two of the four big rivers that feed the Amazon. The waters of the Ucayali have travelled from the hills around distant Lake Titicaca, while the source of the Marañón is near Lima. Pink dolphins gather at the confluence of the rivers, and grey dolphins, considered sacred creatures by many tribes, sometimes

BRING THE CHILDREN

Perfect for families, an astonishing array of wildlife can be viewed from the safety of the boat's observation deck. Some of the more expensive companies, in particular International Expeditions (*www.ietravel.com*), offer cruises tailored to families, with dedicated tour leaders for children, storytelling sessions where Amazonian legends are recounted beneath the stars and even child-friendly menus. Older kids can go canoeing with river dolphins, play football with children they meet at native villages and take music lessons on board.

join in. After lunch, adults visit a local shaman to learn about medicinal plants, while the children board a small launch to look for sloths, monkeys and giant water lilies (*see p106*).

Day 3
The Pacaya Samiria Reserve

Sandwiched between the Ucayali and Marañón rivers is this unique reserve with its flooded forest, shimmering lagoons and twisting tributaries, where giant river otters munch happily on the abundant fish. Go ashore for a walk through the forest and seek out the scarlet macaw and playful spider monkey.

Day 4
The Golden Serpent – **Río Marañón**

The Río Marañón is immortalised in Ciro Alegría's novel *La Serpiente de Oro* (*The Golden Serpent*) (1935), which described the life of the indigenous tribes that lived by the meandering

river. A hero to the Indians, Alegría served two jail terms for his staunch political views. After dusk, take a torchlit walk through the forest to spot poison-dart frogs, and then board a canoe to look for the shining eyes of caimans lurking in the murk.

Day 5
Back to Iquitos

As you sail back down the Amazon, relax with a cocktail and savour your last lingering look at the most important ecological treasure in the world. You can encourage children to write about their experience and draw pictures of their favourite animals. Consider making a regular contribution to help manage and protect the Pacaya Samiria Reserve (visit *www.nature.org*).

Sighting a sloth is a rare treat

Amazon life ... and death

A quarter of the medicinal drugs that are used in the West are derived from rainforest ingredients, yet not even 2 per cent of Amazonian tree and plant species have been thoroughly studied by scientists. Deep in this jungle, cures for many fatal diseases may be locked in microbes that are yet to be discovered. Sadly, 20 per cent of the Amazon jungle has already been

Walking on giant Amazon water lilies

SKYSCRAPERS

As noisy as any city, the jungle teems with life, much of it in the canopy above. The Amazon Canopy Walkway, northwest of Iquitos, is one of the best ways to see the myriad birds, monkeys and lizards that live high in the trees. Over 500m (1,651ft) long, the walkway is slung between 12 giant trees at heights of up to 35m (115ft). Look out for macaws, ospreys, eagles and kites among the hundreds of bird species. The walkway is privately owned, and visits must be arranged as part of an Explorama lodge stay (*www.explorama.com*). This organisation has solid environmental credentials, and guides who are renowned for their experience.

destroyed by farming, logging and oil exploration, and, if we continue on our present course, potential wonder drugs may be lost forever.

Stripping the jungle of its timber and mineral deposits offers no long-term security to the natives, and their best hope lies in carefully managed ecotourism. Choose your lodgings with care because some have a poor track record – one lodge has even created its own artificial 'monkey island' to entertain visitors.

Extreme flora and fauna

Wherever you venture in Peru's vast Amazon basin, you will be surrounded by an astonishing array of plant, animal, bird and insect species. Some are easier to spot than others, but eagle-eyed local guides will generally point you in the right direction.

You won't need a guide to spot the Amazon water lily (*Victoria regia*). Over 2.5m (8ft) in diameter, it can support the weight of a child. When the botanist Thaddaeus Haenke came across it in 1801, he reportedly fell to his knees in admiration. Another botanist, Alcide d'Orbigny, said, 'It is without any exception, if we take it as a whole – leaves, flowers, size, colour, and graceful position in the water, especially when viewed with the usual accompaniments of Tropical American aquatic scenery – the most beautiful plant known to Europeans.'

With patience and luck, you may be rewarded with sightings of elusive mammals such as jaguars and tapirs, while the gregarious giant river otter is almost guaranteed. Pink dolphins are a common sight where two rivers join, and the world's largest – and perhaps most frightened – rodent, the capybara, makes its home here, hunted by vultures on land and by piranha in the river.

Reptiles such as river turtles and the fearsome caiman, a relative of the alligator, can usually be spotted in the water, while gigantic anacondas cling to branches above. On land, boas and vipers skulk through the

The colourful scarlet macaw stands out in the Amazon greenery

undergrowth. Most snakes will not attack humans, but there are exceptions. The poisonous *shushupe* (Amazon bushmaster), up to 3.5m (11ft) long, has been known to stalk humans by their scent. Many natives have died from its bites.

THE SOUTHERN JUNGLE

Much of Peru's inaccessible jungle survived intact well into the 20th century, but in latter years more and more areas came under threat from oil exploration and mining. Fortunately, the Peruvian government has seen the light, and there are some well-protected national parks in the south. Visitors generally fly into Puerto Maldonado or directly to Manu to start their jungle adventure.

The national bird, the glorious cock-of-the-rock

Manu Biosphere Reserve

The park is divided into three: most of it is out of bounds to humans, a small part is given over to scientific research and guided tours, and the remainder is home to some native Indian settlements. The sheer scale of this reserve, and the strict controls on tourism, make a trip here expensive – annually, around 3,000 visitors come here compared with the 20,000 who head to the jungle around Puerto Maldonado.

Manu contains 13 different ecological zones, some as high as 4,000m (13,000ft), and the variety of life on show is astounding. Highlights are the rare emperor tamarin monkey with its long white moustache, and the endangered spectacled bear – the only species of bear in South America. Here too is Peru's national bird, the bright red cock-of-the-rock, whose noisy mating display is sure to draw attention. The trails through the cloud forest feel almost prehistoric,

so untouched are they by the modern world. On the banks of the Río Manu, jaguars sometimes sunbathe, and the river has given birth to 13 oxbow lakes (cut off from the river's flow as it meanders around), the largest of which is Cocha Salvador – a perfect place for waterside camping beneath the stars.

Parque Nacional Bahuaja-Sonene

This relatively new park spans the border with Bolivia. Within is the Heath River Wildlife Centre (six hours by boat from Puerto Maldonado), which is owned by the indigenous Ese Eja people. Red howler monkeys chase each other through the trees, and, at the nearby clay lick, parrots and macaws gather each morning for a detox session – the lumps of mineral-rich clay they eat from the river bank counter the poisons in their rainforest diet of seeds and nuts. All profits support the local community, and the lodge is constructed entirely of sustainable timber.

Heath River Wildlife Centre. Book through www.tropicalnaturetravel.com

Puerto Maldonado

This rapidly expanding frontier town is of little interest, except as a staging point for transfer to lodges in the Tambopata-Candamo and Bahuaja-Sonene reserves. There are daily flights from Lima (two hours) and Cusco (30 minutes). It's also possible to get here by truck from Cusco, but the rough three-day journey is only for die-hards. The uncomfortable boats into Manu from Puerto Maldonado can take anything from six to twelve hours, so fly direct from Cusco instead.

Zona Reservada Tambopata-Candamo

More accessible than Manu, and cheaper, this reserve is spread over 890,034ha (2.2 million acres) of primary forest south of Puerto Maldonado. A number of lodges operate in the reserve – some within a few kilometres of the town, others up to eight hours away (*see p171*). Lodge stays should be booked in advance from Cusco or Lima – look for good deals that include connecting flights. The reserve holds numerous world records for biodiversity. Among the 550 bird species is the harpy eagle, an accomplished predator of sloths, anteaters and even howler monkeys.

The Amazon

This 'oxbow' lake in Manu was orphaned from the river – cut off by the jungle at a tight bend in the waterway

The north coast

Squeezed between some of the richest fishing grounds in the world and some of its highest mountains, this thin strip of land was the centre for several pre-Inca civilisations. It is Peru's least-visited area, a barren, desert region that is nonetheless sprinkled with some of the most important archaeological sites in the Americas. Visit the towering pyramids of the Sun and the Moon temples, the glittering Sipán tomb that rivals King Tutankhamun's, and Chán Chán – the largest adobe (hard, dried mud) city in the world.

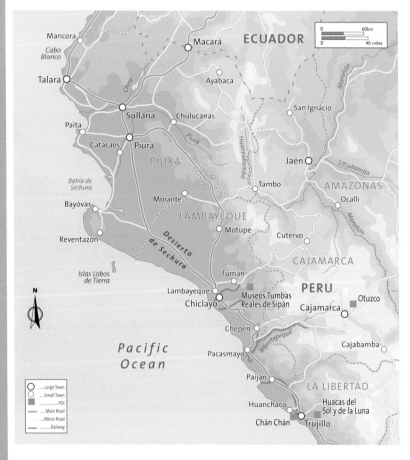

Enjoying beach life at Mancora

The coastal settlements of Trujillo, Huanchaco and Chiclayo provide good bases from which to explore the north coast's history. Approaching the border with Ecuador is the old Ernest Hemingway haunt of Cabo Blanco, and the surfers' hang-out of Mancora.

The archaeological sites are best visited as part of a tour. Not only does this make the travelling easier, but since there is often little that is obvious to the untrained eye, and even less signed information, a decent guide is a must. Those determined to travel independently can take one of the many *collectivos* (minibuses), or preferably a taxi, and then hire a guide on arrival. Many of the sites are in out-of-the-way locations; for this reason, women are not advised to travel on their own and no one should stray from the paths.

If you are intending to visit more than one of the sites mentioned, consider going on a tour over several days that can take you to all of the main sites in this region. Trips can be tailored to meet individual interests and need not be expensive. Whichever way you decide to travel, the sites in this area are best visited in the morning, avoiding the heat of the midday sun and the afternoon winds that can whip up the sand.

Trujillo, Huanchaco and Chiclayo

Each of these north-coast settlements is ideal as a springboard to the surrounding archaeological sites. Trujillo, Peru's third-largest city with a historical centre and a number of *casas colonials* (colonial houses), is only a short distance from the Huacas del Sol y de la Luna and Chán Chán. Nearby Huanchaco is a relaxed, traditional fishing village, while, further north, Chiclayo has a colourful local market and is convenient for the Sipán museum. If visiting the region, which is the birthplace of *ceviche*, make sure to sample this delicious fish dish marinated with lime and chilli, and also find time to experience a performance of the local Marinera dance.

The prows of upended reed fishing boats on the beach at Huanchaco

Chiclayo

Chiclayo is 200km (124 miles) north of Trujillo. It is a modern, busy city, with a cluster of ancient churches and a cathedral. The locals are friendly and it is a good place to meet Peruvians away from the more touristy centres. The main reason to come here, though, is as a base for visits to the nearby tomb of Sipán.

Huanchaco

This low-key fishing village, a suburb 12km (7¹/₂ miles) northeast of Trujillo, is developing at a rapid pace. Swimming isn't good from the beach here, but do make sure you catch sight of the fishermen setting out on their unique reed vessels known as *caballitos* (little horses). These boats have such a long history that they appear on Moche pottery and on friezes at Chán Chán.

Trujillo's colonial main square

THE OLD MAN AND THE SEA

Some local tourist offices like to claim that Peru was Ernest Hemingway's inspiration for his novel *The Old Man and the Sea* (1952). It was in fact Cuba, but there is another story that does ring true: before the film of Hemingway's novel was shot (1958), starring Spencer Tracy, the prize-winning novelist ran off to Peru's Cabo Blanco to fish for a huge marlin to appear in the production; in the end a rubber fish was used. Cabo Blanco had a glamorous reputation in the 1950s, which has sadly long since faded. However, the fishing club still holds several world records and surfers maintain this beach spot has the best left-breaking wave in the country.

Trujillo

Avenida España conveniently circles the city centre, creating an easily recognisable colonial core. Here, there are colourful mansions with elegant balconies and courtyards, and historic churches (*all with erratic opening times, but best visited on weekday mornings*). La Casa Urquiaga on the south side of the Plaza de Armas is one of the most impressive houses, and was once home to the liberator Simón Bolívar. As is the case in so many other cities in Peru, the cathedral (18th century, with a small museum) is in the main square of the Plaza de Armas. One block south is the splendid Casona Orbegoso, where the former president Luis José de Orbegoso once lived. It now functions partly as a cultural centre. The neoclassical 19th-century Palacio Iturregui, two blocks east of the main square, is now home to a social club, but its ornate features can be viewed from the outside.

Excursion: Chán Chán

The capital of the Chimú kingdom was the largest city in pre-Columbian South America and is a UNESCO World Heritage Site. Covering an area of 28sq km (11sq miles), Chán Chán in its heyday housed as many as 50,000 people. The Chimú appeared on Peru's coast in AD 1000 and reached their zenith in the 13th century before surrendering to the Incas in the 15th century. Descendants of the Moche, the Chimú people called the city Jang Jang, meaning 'Sun Sun'; it became Chán Chán under Spanish rule.

Palace compounds

Chán Chán is built entirely of adobe (hard, dried mud). Walls 12m (39ft) high once surrounded the complex, which was divided into ten enormous palace compounds. Each contained temples, gardens and plazas connected by narrow corridors, and rooms where it is thought only the aristocracy lived; commoners lived outside the main complex walls. Each king had his own citadel, where he lived and stored his wealth. When a king died, he was buried on a platform with all his treasures and often several hundred human sacrifices – his residence became his mausoleum, with the succeeding king moving on to build his own, new compound and final resting place.

The adobe city of Chán Chán

Sophisticated society

The Chimú society operated as a strict hierarchy with political leaders who were well organised. Canals brought water from the Andes, which irrigated the crops in deep sunken gardens. The pottery was highly decorative, and the Chimú people were skilled goldsmiths. They carved elaborate friezes depicting geometric shapes and animals in the walls of Chán Chán that can still be seen today. There are three main sites spread over a large area; tickets for all are sold at the Tschudi Palace (*see below*). If you want to see more than the walls and structures from a distance, be prepared to do a lot of walking and to pay for a couple of taxi rides.

The ornate walls of the Tschudi Palace

two platforms (the higher of which offers panoramic views), walls and pathways. Sadly, the decorated walls were severely damaged in freak rains. *Chán Chán. Open: 9am–5.30pm. Last entry: 4pm. Admission charge.*

La Huaca Arco Iris (The Rainbow Temple)

Also called the Huaca del Dragón, this temple 4km (2½ miles) north of Trujillo is the best-preserved ruin within Chán Chán as it was uncovered only in the 1960s. Ramps lead up to the top of the temple, whose walls display rainbow and dragon friezes. Strange Peruvian hairless dogs (*perro sin pelo del Perú*) may join you on your tour.
Chán Chán. Open: 9am–5.30pm. Last entry: 4pm. Admission charge.

La Huaca Esmeralda (The Emerald Temple)

This beautiful temple 2km (1¼ miles) from Tschudi on the edge of Trujillo was part of a complex that included

Tschudi Palace

If you see only one of the three sites in Chán Chán, make it this one. The palace houses a small museum and the ticket office. One ticket (valid for two days) allows you to see this and the two sites listed above, but you must buy it here. Tschudi is the most fully restored palace compound and the only one where visitors are allowed inside. Enter through the 4m (13ft) thick wall and then follow the arrows. The main features to look out for are the ceremonial courtyard with its aquatic-themed friezes, the sanctuary where 'fishnets' have been hewn out of the walls, and the funerary platform where the Chimú king was placed, surrounded by his concubines, guards and officials.
Chán Chán. Open: 9am–5.30pm. Last entry: 4pm. Admission charge.

Temples and tombs of the Moche Valley

The Moche people were farmers and fishermen who lived in the valley of Lambayeque from AD 100 to 700. They began to occupy the north of Peru after the decline of the Chavín and were superseded by the Chimú culture. Like the other pre-Columbian cultures, the Moche did not have a written language, expressing themselves instead through their pottery, which displayed sophisticated images of daily and religious life. It is the Moche who are responsible for the highly erotic pieces on display in the Museo Arqueológico Rafael Larco Herrera in Lima (*see p32*) and others throughout the country.

A skeleton-filled Moche tomb

Huacas del Sol y de la Luna (Temples of the Sun and Moon)

Rising out of a dusty plain next to the 'White Mountain' 13km (8 miles) southeast of Trujillo are the two enormous stepped pyramids of the Huacas del Sol y de la Luna (Temples of the Sun and Moon). Part of a city of mud that formed the Moche capital, the site was first battered by the desert winds and then severely damaged by the Spanish, who diverted the Santa Catalina River so that it washed away at least half of the constructions.

The 48m (158ft) high Huaca del Sol stands 200m (220yds) away from the slightly smaller Huaca de la Luna, originally made from 140 million sun-dried mud bricks (or adobes). Many of these bricks still bear images, such as feet and crosses, that are thought to indicate their source for tax purposes. The area between the two temples was a bustling industrial and agricultural district, where ceramics were made and Chica beer produced; nearby hundreds of kilometres of irrigation canals were built to water the parched land.

The whole centre is made up of a series of platforms and plazas connected by narrow corridors and dotted with burial grounds. Over time, structures were filled in to make new ones, which accounts for its size. Finds here include human sacrifices as well as highly decorative ceramics and headwear. Some friezes on the walls remain, showing geometric shapes and images of frightening animals.
Open: 9am–4pm. Admission charge.

Museos Tumbas Reales de Sipán (Royal Tombs of Sipán Museum)

One of the most important archaeological discoveries in recent years was made on the edge of Chiclayo in the town of Lambayeque in 1987. This was the discovery of the spectacular tomb of the Lord of Sipán, a warrior priest who was a direct descendant of the Moche and is thought to have died around AD 250. The gold found buried with him, numbering more than 1,000 items, including jewellery encrusted with precious gems, is the largest discovery of intact gold pieces in the Americas. Similar to the effect of the earth-shattering discovery of the tomb of Tutankhamun in Egypt, it led to a much better understanding of the Moche culture.

Sipán's head was laid on a large gold plate, his face covered with gold ornaments, and on his feet a pair of silver shoes. His wives and most favoured warriors, and his guard with mutilated feet – symbolising his eternal duty to stand his post – were buried with him. Also in the tomb were numerous gold ceremonial objects, including knives, nose-plates and goblets, encrusted with precious jewels. Later, two other tombs, those of the Old Lord of Sipán and the Priest, were found nearby.

Visitors can experience the finds in the order in which the archaeologists discovered them, thanks to a spectacular three-storey museum. It was built in the shape of a pyramid that visitors enter through the roof.
Avenida Juan Pablo Vizcardo y Guzmán. Tel: (074) 283 977. www. museosipan.com (Spanish only). Open: Tue–Sun 9am–5pm. Admission charge.

The intricately decorated interior of the Temple of the Moon

Grave robbers:
the Peruvian gold rush

Archaeologists in Peru have a hard time piecing together their country's complicated and fascinating history. Mostly, this is the fault of *huaqueros* (literally, 'robbers of temples') who have come in many guises and from all over the world. First came the Spanish conquistadors, and later the American explorer Hiram Bingham (*see p72*), who plundered Machu Picchu, and more recently the impoverished Peruvian *huaqueros*. Even today, Peru is quite literally being robbed of its heritage.

The final resting place of the Lord of Sipán

European gold diggers

When the Incas conquered the Chimú, they left Chán Chán and its treasures more or less intact. Soon after, in the mid-1530s, the Spanish arrived and removed huge piles of precious treasure. It was their standard *modus operandi* and they repeated it throughout South America until the 18th century, often with the help of organised companies and always with the permission of the Spanish Crown.

The gentleman thief

After Hiram Bingham 'discovered' Machu Picchu in 1911, intellectuals managed to push through a decree forbidding the exportation of any Peruvian antiquities. Bingham brazenly dismissed this as petty jealousy and shipped back to Yale, at the National Geographic Society's request, items ranging from jewellery to human remains. This represents the only intact collection from an Incan royal state to escape the grasp of the Spanish, yet for nearly 100 years Yale has refused to return the finds, and now the Peruvian government is threatening to sue.

Midnight robbery

In 1987, police woke archaeologist Dr Walter Alva in the middle of the night to tell him that a new tomb had been discovered – by grave robbers. The tomb was at Sipán and 20 sacks of artefacts had already disappeared when Alva arrived at the scene. Horrified, he watched as *huaqueros* swarmed over the temple mounds, gripped by a kind of gold fever. Peru was in economic crisis and these impoverished locals believed their ancestors' treasure was their rightful property. The *huaquero* who discovered the royal tombs of Sipán did not enjoy Hiram Bingham's fame and fortune – he died from gunshots fired by the police.

The international market

Some experts point to a kind of pre-Columbian art pyramid, with the poor *huaqueros* at the bottom providing goods to the world's wealthiest countries at its apex. Peruvian treasure regularly turns up around the world – in the UK, Germany, Japan and the USA, although the Peruvian government has made some headway in cracking down on a trade estimated to be worth £400 million each year. In September 2006, a prized 1,300-year-old gold headdress featuring an elaborate feline face was returned 'home'. Taken in 1988 from

A *tumi* – masterpiece of Mochica metalwork

a tomb in the Jequetepeque Valley of northern Peru, it is now in Lima's Museo de la Nación (National Museum, *see p32*).

A token of good luck

As recently as November 2006 in Ferrenafe, northern Peru, a hoard of pre-Inca artefacts was discovered in 22 graves, wholly untouched by robbers. The most exciting finds are the first *tumis* (ceremonial knives) ever to be scientifically excavated rather than looted. This allows scientists to study the historical context and significance of the *tumi*, which is not only a token of good luck but Peru's national symbol.

Getting away from it all

On a visit to Peru, it is tempting to dash from one archaeological hot spot to another. The likes of Cusco, Machu Picchu and the Nazca Lines must be seen, but it can be rewarding to take a detour from the usual tourist trail. Whether it's on the beaches around Lima where weekend surfers hang out, or in the mountains around Cusco where Quechua farmers eke a small living from the land, there are unexpected opportunities for gaining a deeper understanding of the country's culture.

While the Colca Canyon is on everyone's list when visiting Arequipa, the Cotahuasi is deeper and more remote, with hiking, rafting and wildlife that is unforgettable. In the central Andes, everyone heads to Huaraz to explore the Huascarán National Park, but further south are the dramatic and challenging hikes of the Cordillera Huayhuash, awash with glacial lakes but devoid of people.

In the north, most visitors get only as far as Trujillo on the coast, but inland is a wondrous landscape of paddy fields,

Escape to the wildest parts of Peru, such as the Huayhuash in the central Andes

fertile hills and startling rock formations, not to mention some important pre-Inca and Inca ruins, and picturesque colonial towns such as Cajamarca.

Some of the options here can be fitted in to a busy holiday, where there is just a day or two to spare, while others might need four days, a week or more. Try to make some time to get off the beaten track, and spend a while meeting the Peruvians who don't see many tourists – enjoy their genuine hospitality, warmth and unspoiled way of life.

Beaches around Lima

After a brief stay in Lima's historic centre, most visitors shoot off to tourist centres such as Cusco, but if you have a day or two to spare you can head out of Lima to some of the relaxed beaches that are within a day's drive of the centre and offer great swimming and surfing opportunities.

Just 40 minutes from the centre of Lima is La Herradura (The Horseshoe), with its world-class left-breaking surf, and chilled-out restaurants known as *picanterías*. Further south (130km/ 81 miles from Lima) is Cerro Azul (Blue Hill), a popular summer getaway with Limeños. The long pier here was built by a British company in 1900 when Azul was a busy cotton port. The last ship docked in 1971, and now the place is left to surfers and fishermen. Waves lap the sandy beach around the pier, where animated locals discuss the day's events among their colourfully

Fishing boats at Cerro Azul

painted fishing boats. At the head of the beach is a dramatic point where rocks jut out against the surf, immortalised in the Beach Boys' 'Surfin' Safari'. At the south end of the beach is Centiela Hill, where pre-Hispanic ruins can still be seen.

There is a great swimming beach 200km (124 miles) from Lima, near the town of Puerto Supe. Its name, El Faraón (The Pharaoh), comes from the pyramid-shaped island just offshore. Locals know to swim the 30m (33yds) out to the island, where a scenic lagoon offers calm waters and beautiful views. After a day on the beach, head into Supe, where there are plenty of inexpensive *ceviche* (fish marinated with lime and chilli) restaurants.

Riding at the base of the Cotahuasi Canyon

Cotahuasi Canyon

Travellers to Arequipa are attracted to the Colca Canyon with its dramatic views and the chance to spot condors in flight. Yet the same and more is on offer at the less-visited Cotahuasi Canyon (*see map, p79*). This is arguably the deepest canyon in the world at 3,354m (11,004ft) but what is not in doubt is that the hiking here is a fantastic experience. Trekking into the gorge takes a good two days, but the sense of splendid isolation makes it worthwhile.

Hundreds of different trails meander down and through the canyon, crossing the gorge by simple suspended rope bridges that offer stunning views of the Río Cotahuasi below. This watercourse, with hundreds of kilometres of torrential Class IV and V rapids, is just beginning to be discovered by rafting enthusiasts.

Not even world-class rafters would attempt the Sipia waterfalls (over 30m/98ft high), but for the hiker this scenic cascade is just one of many to be found along the hike. The village of Cotahuasi, with its relaxing hot springs, is at the head of the canyon and is the starting and end point for most hikes. Aim to spend a minimum of three days in the canyon, perhaps opting to travel some parts on horseback or mule to give your feet a rest. Expect very basic lodgings, or bring camping gear.

The canyon is 200km (124 miles) northwest of Arequipa, at least 14 hours' drive, partly on dirt tracks.

Hiking in Huayhuash

The Cordillera Huayhuash lies 50km (31 miles) south of the well-travelled Cordillera Blanca, on the border with the Huánuco region (*see map, p48*). This region is difficult to access, and much of the route is close to 5,000m (16,405ft) and arduous, so mules and guides are recommended. Visitors should plan on spending eight to twelve days here, beginning and ending in the town of Chiquián.

Within the Huayhuash are many glacial lakes, such as Laguna Conococha – the source of the Río Santa, which becomes the Amazon near the jungle town of Iquitos (*see p102*). Soaring skywards are giant peaks such as Yerupaja (6,634m/21,766ft) and Siula Grande (6,356m/20,854ft), the latter made famous by *Touching the Void* – a harrowing tale of a young British mountaineer, Joe Simpson, who struggled to descend the peak alone with a broken leg. The region is home to small herds of llama, vicuña and alpaca, and, at such heights, it is not unusual to see condors soaring on the thermals. There are a few villages along the route, such as Llamac and Pocpa, where hospitable locals will brew coca tea (*mate de coca*) for tired hikers, but other than that it's just you and mother nature.

Chiquián is a 2-hour drive from the town of Huaraz, or 3 hours by bus. December to March in Huayhuash is marked by heavy rains, while May to October is dry and sunny, but with very cold nights.

A string of remote lagoons in the Cordillera Huayhuash

Staying with a Quechua family

For a change from the well-worn path trodden by most visitors to Peru, why not spend one or two nights staying with a Quechua family, either in the highlands near Cusco or on one of Lake Titicaca's island havens? This will generally involve sharing a very basic family home, helping to prepare meals, tending the family's crops and domestic animals, and of course getting to know the family. As accommodation goes, this will be one of your least expensive options, but more important will be the rewards, for you and for the family you stay with.

Around Cusco

Non-profit Andean Travel Web operates a highly recommended homestay scheme. For a small fee, it will arrange meals and accommodation with a

A host's simple home on Taquile, Lake Titicaca

family in the village of Chinchero, an hour's drive from Cusco. Spend your first evening drinking coca tea (*mate de coca*) around the fire, while listening to Quechua and Inca legends. Next morning, help with the llamas and visit the locals' market to buy that evening's meal. Charges for meals and lodging are more than reasonable, with all money paid direct to the family. *www.andeantravelweb.com/peru/projects/quechua_homestays.html*

On Lake Titicaca

The islanders of Taquile and Amantaní (*see p95*) offer their own homestays where all money goes directly to the villagers. Both islands are a few hours from the port of Puno, with Amantaní more remote, and consequently less visited. On both islands, the sense of communal spirit is tangible – it is humbling to see how well families cooperate, ensuring that all the fields are well irrigated, the crops shared out fairly, and the children looked after. Try to spend at least two nights here, away from the crowds around the floating islands near Puno.

Trips can be booked from hotels and hostels in Puno, but it is better and cheaper to go directly to the dock and find some boatmen from the island.

The unexplored north: Cajamarca

Almost 300km (186 miles) from the northern coastal city of Trujillo is this historic highland getaway, surrounded by lush countryside and

The stone forest of Los Frailones near Cajamarca

rich in Incan ruins and extraordinary remnants of even earlier civilisations (*see map, p110*).

In the city centre is the Cuarto del Rescate (Ransom Room). Here, the Inca Atahualpa, having been captured by Francisco Pizarro, stood with his arms upstretched and marked the height on the wall. He offered to fill the room up to the mark, once with gold and twice with silver, in exchange for his release. Pizarro took the ransom, then had Atahualpa executed. To the east of the city is the Baños del Inca, a complex of natural hot springs popular with the Inca nobles.

The Ventanillas de Otuzco, 8km (5 miles) northeast of the city, is a fascinating complex of burial caves carved out of solid rock by the Caxamarca people who predated the Incas. The Caxamarca are also responsible for Cumbe Mayo, 21km

(13 miles) southwest of the city. This is a huge archaeological site containing fortresses, caves and beautifully constructed stone aqueducts. Nearby is a striking group of rocks sprouting from the plain, which the Spanish thought resembled a group of friars in procession, and so named it Los Frailones.

Undoubtedly, the best time to visit Cajamarca is during Carnival, as the locals celebrate perhaps more enthusiastically than anywhere else in Peru. Almost the whole month (usually February or March) is taken up with feasts, singing competitions, beauty pageants, marches and dances, and there is even a competition to find the best-dressed car.

To get to Cajamarca, the day-long bus ride from Trujillo is a scenic option, or alternatively visitors can fly in from Lima – just over 1 hour.

When to go

Peru's seasons are the reverse of those in the northern hemisphere. Generally speaking, summer is from December to February, and winter between July and September, but there are many variations within that. Unless you are planning a particular outdoor activity, there is not a bad time to visit Peru.

Fair weather

As a very loose recommendation, the summer is the best time to visit the coast and the winter the mountains. Most tourists – both foreign and

For a real mountain adventure, visit in winter

Peruvian – travel in winter (July to September).

To avoid crowds and higher prices in hotels and restaurants, consider visiting outside of these months.

Coastal climate

The desert coast enjoys long, hot summers between December and April with little or even no rain. Temperatures rise the higher up the coast you travel, but even here it can get chilly and misty in winter. Lima has its own microclimate, and from June to October is frequently blanketed in a heavy fog. Don't expect warm waters for swimming; the freezing Humboldt Current means the ocean off the coast of Peru doesn't heat up much. Every decade or so in December or January, El Niño makes an appearance, slamming into the coast and sometimes wreaking devastation, washing over roads and destroying houses.

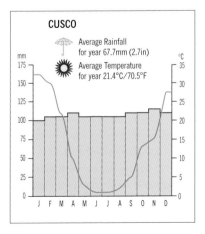

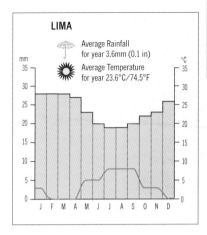

When to go

WEATHER CONVERSION CHART

25.4mm = 1 inch
°F = 1.8 × °C + 32

Active tourism

Mountain trekkers and climbers should aim to travel in winter, which lasts from July until September. During these months it is cold but also fairly dry; severe rains from December to March can hamper activities. Rafters, on the other hand, should opt for the rainy season, when 'white waters' appear.

The jungle areas are relentlessly hot and steamy all year round, with heavy rains in December and January. This is the best time for visitors hoping to see animals, because the higher water levels allow canoe access to side creeks rich in wildlife.

Getting around

When planning your trip to Peru, remember that this is a country split down the middle by the second-highest mountain range in the world. Always consider the need for acclimatisation when moving from low to high altitude. Most people will need to spend a day or two at around 3,000m (10,000ft) before going higher, and, if you are planning to hike, allow extra time to cope with the exhaustion caused by the thin mountain air.

In the big cities, expect gridlock at peak times, and adjust journey times accordingly. When planning long trips and excursions, be prepared for delays and cancellations – the infrastructure here is not the worst in the world, but the weather, transport strikes and overbooking can all impact on your trip. The best thing to do is relax and enjoy the ride, and don't get too attached to your itinerary.

By air

In many cases, air travel is the only way to go. Not only is Peru big, but the long, high spine of the Andes can make much of the country impenetrable; travelling over these mountains by bus, or even private car, is a long, bumpy ride. Planes, too, are really the only practical way to get to the jungle. Every destination in Peru is within a two-hour flight from Lima. LAN Peru (*www.lan.com*) offers the most comprehensive choice of domestic flights.

Private air tours

Those with deep pockets and a hectic schedule can choose to see Machu Picchu by helicopter, or even hire a private plane. Unistar (*www.unistar.com.pe*) has a number of different packages to choose from, any one of which would make for an unforgettable journey.

By bicycle

Even if you are very fit, most of Peru is hostile terrain for cyclists, and cycle hire is available only in a few tourist hot spots such as Cusco and Arequipa. Long expanses of featureless desert highway connect the coastal towns and cities, which means that you must carry a heavy load of food and water. Travelling into the highlands and across the Altiplano is even more gruelling – places to rest, eat and sleep are few and far between, and temperatures range from blisteringly hot during the day to bitterly cold in the early morning and after sundown.

This said, cycling can be a great way to explore the surroundings of Cusco and Arequipa or regions such as the Cordillera Blanca or the Colca Canyon, where mountain bikes can be hired locally.

By boat

When it comes to getting around the jungle, this is the way to travel if you want to see some fascinating wildlife without the bone-crunching treks that this can often involve. River cruises from Iquitos are a popular option, where passengers spend five or more days sailing upriver in comparative luxury (*see p104*).

Those staying at jungle lodges will still want to take to the river to access remote lagoons, to spot caimans on the river bank at night, and to get up close to pink river dolphins. On Lake Titicaca, boats are an obvious essential, ferrying passengers to the

Travelling by rail offers breathtaking views

islands, and for those who just want to skirt the shoreline in the search of rare birds.

By bus

If Peruvians need to travel, it is generally by bus, which is usually the cheapest option. Buses are run by a number of different companies, and as a result the information available can be confusing. Local buses stop often and are uncomfortable, and the few tourists who travel on them are often targeted by thieves. At the other end of the spectrum, luxury coach companies provide food, films and even beds. Most companies offer at least two classes – you won't pay much more for the higher ones and it is usually well worth it.

Mototaxis – motorised rickshaws – are often used

Because of the terrain, journeys can be long and hard. While coaches zip up and down the main artery of the coastal highway, zigzagging over the mountains can be bone-rattling and take an age, with punctures, driver disputes and landslides common. Bus travel in the jungle is even worse. In either case, avoid a seat over the wheels. Longer bus journeys are often scheduled overnight, but if you don't want to miss the scenery it is possible to make shorter journeys by day.

By car

Driving is another option, although not one you would want to consider in Lima, where daily gridlock is the norm. The Panamericana (Pan-American Highway) runs the full length of the coast and is one of the few roads that is consistently paved and in good condition. Those considering driving in Peru should be prepared for unstable motorists as well as unpredictable weather – landslides caused by flooding often close roads. One particularly interesting route takes in the highlights of the south coast (*see p44*). Driving through the mountains or jungle is not recommended. For longer journeys, a taxi can be rented for anything from a few hours to a few weeks.

Taxis

Taxis are easy to come by and very reasonably priced. Tips are not necessary, but of course greatly appreciated. Only take a ride with an official taxi and always fix a price before setting off (ask at your hotel for a price guide). Radio taxis, found in larger towns and cities, have meters and are more reliable, although they are more expensive and must be booked by telephone in advance. In rural areas, motor rickshaws can be hired – great for a novel journey and if you have kids, but not if you have a lot of luggage. *Collectivos* (minibuses) are a kind of cross between a taxi and a bus – in terms of both price and speed.

By train

Visitors should try to travel by train at least once – for example, to Machu Picchu or to Lake Titicaca (*see pp68 and 76*) – not for speed, but for a memorable journey through spectacular scenery. For more information, go to PeruRail's website (*www.perurail.com*).

Access for travellers with disabilities

Peru does not have very well-developed services for travellers with disabilities, although the government has made a commitment to improve this. Hotels, tourist attractions and toilets rarely have ramps or handrails. However, there are specialist agencies, such as Perucusco (*www.perucusco.com*), that can arrange travel, as well as a handful of hotels with disabled facilities, including those that are part of the Sonesta chain (*www.sonesta.com*).

Accommodation

Bear in mind that a 'five-star' hotel does not invariably mean what it does at home – in terms of service, your laid-back South American location will probably take precedence over any rating. Ask yourself whether a TV, telephone and minibar are really what you want from your trip to Peru. Consider staying with a local family, in Cusco for example, in order to gain a deeper understanding of the indigenous culture. Such homestays are available in rural areas (see p124), but increasingly in urban regions too.

Take your pick

At the higher end of the scale, opt for one of Peru's grand and historic hotels, places of interest in their own right. If you can't stretch to a room in one of these colonial palaces, pop in for tea, a cocktail or dinner, and savour the old-world atmosphere at a fraction of the cost. The elegant five-star Monasterio Hotel in Cusco was built as a monastery in the 16th century on the foundations of an Inca palace. Today, it is part of the Orient Express group, with a lovely bar and two restaurants open to non-residents (*see p167*). In Lima, the stately Gran Hotel Bolívar (*www.granhotelbolivarperu.com*) was built in the 1920s to receive guests of honour celebrating the centennial of the Peruvian republic. A drink on the terrace is a must.

Business hotels can be found in all the major towns and cities throughout the country. A mid-range option for visitors, these do have a tendency to be functional, and even drab. Guesthouses are the norm in smaller towns and rural areas. Developed camping facilities are nonexistent in Peru, but you can pitch your tent at designated spots along the Inca Trail, or in Peru's national parks (subject to registration and restrictions). There are hostels in all of the main tourist areas, generally with private rooms as well as dormitories. Facilities and cleanliness are variable, but most are keenly priced and a good place to meet other travellers. Note that *hostal* does not translate as 'hostel', but can refer to any small hotel.

Those with children or with a fondness for self-catering may want to choose a suite or apartment. They are available in Lima through companies such as Hoteles Las Americas (*www.hoteleslasamericas.com*).

In the Amazon, standard accommodation is in a lodge, up on stilts away from the encroaching flood waters and ground scavengers. The alternative is a tour boat, sleeping in a hammock at the low price end, or in a well-appointed cabin at the high price end. Moving around this way maximises your wildlife-spotting options and is a good choice for those with children.

To book or not to book?

It is advisable to reserve a room during the peak season, which runs from July to September. Booking accommodation is easy from home or even on the road as most establishments have websites allowing advance booking and confirmation by email. Peru's online tourist office (*www.peru.info*) features a searchable directory for all kinds of accommodation. Although by no means exhaustive, it links directly to hotel sites rather than to accommodation agencies that may add on an extra fee.

All accommodation prices are subject to 19 per cent tax (IGV). Hotels in the higher categories might also add a 10–13 per cent service charge. Try to tip all staff from the porter to the cleaner – they are paid very little, and the price of a coffee at home could well pay for their family meal.

The Country Club Lima Hotel

Food and drink

There may be only several hundred Peruvian restaurants worldwide, but a quiet revolution is changing international perceptions of the country's cuisine. A new breed of creative chefs is cooking up Novo Andino (New Andean) dishes, giving a contemporary twist to traditional food. Peru's 'native' cooking, criolla, *is a mixture of cuisines – Spanish, indigenous and, because of the slave trade, African. Criolla stews and soups are traditionally made with* cuy *(guinea pig) and alpaca.*

Staples

The country's varied geography and climate mean there is a wide range of home-grown crops. Rice, potatoes, corn and, in the jungle, yucca fill the stomachs of most rural Peruvians. Quinoa is an ancient, protein-rich grain grown in the Andes that has recently been discovered by health-food fanatics across the globe. The potato, with more than 100 varieties grown throughout Peru, is the main vegetable, with most others used simply as decoration. Vegetarian restaurants do exist, but only really in the cities of Cusco and Lima. Non-meat options, such as the famous *pallares* salad with Lima beans, tomatoes and chilli, can be found on most menus but can become monotonous fairly quickly.

Foreign and fast food

Thanks to the large immigrant population, there have always been a large number of *chifas* (Chinese restaurants), as well as African and Italian eateries. International fast-food chains do not really exist outside Lima. If you want to eat and run, try *chodo* (corn on the cob), *antichuchos* (spicy, marinated cow's heart) or *cau-cau* (made from cow's stomach and served in a yellow sauce). *Empanadas* (beef, chicken or vegetable pies) are a kind of mini Peruvian Cornish pasty and the continent's favourite fast food.

Meat

Hungry carnivores will find no shortage of delicious meat dishes on offer. *Arroz con pollo* (rice with chicken), *chicharrones* (deep-fried, salted pork) and *lomo saltado* (sautéed beef with onion and tomato) can be found on almost every street corner. *Carapulcra* is a typical Peruvian stew made with pork, chicken, dried potatoes and chilli; *sancochado* is a beef, yucca and sweet potato casserole. Another popular stew, but not to all tastes, is *cau cau* – a concoction of tripe and vegetables.

Fish

Ceviche is raw fish marinated in lime juice. As well as being delicious, it is one of the few hangover 'cures' that actually works. For cooked fish, try *corvina a la plancha* (grilled sea bass) or *chupe de camerones* (prawn and vegetables in a thick creamy soup). Where available, fresh *mariscos* (seafood) is generally excellent – try *choros a la chalaca*, a dish of mussels and peppers in vinaigrette. If you're looking for fish, have it for lunch, like the locals. The best of the morning's catch is sold before then, and, in fact, many fish restaurants close around 6pm.

A bit of sauce

Peruvian food is not generally hot and spicy, but can be made so with the addition of *salsa picante* (spicy sauce), a condiment found on almost all restaurant tables. Don't confuse *salsa* with the Mexican side dish of tomatoes and onions – here it is any kind of sauce.

Desserts

Desserts tend to be very sweet and made with sweetened condensed milk – a result of the Spanish and Arab influence on Peru. While *arroz con leche* (rice with milk) is everywhere, *suspiro de Limeña* (sigh of a woman from

Expect simple, rice-based dishes, made with fresh local ingredients

A cup of coca tea can ease altitude sickness

Lima) is probably the classic *criolla* dessert – a sweet-milk caramel with meringue and cinnamon that melts in the mouth. Another popular *postre* (dessert) is *picarones* – ring doughnuts made with yam and soaked in molasses. Aside from these, the wonderful variety of exotic fruits found here features heavily on dessert menus.

Cost

Tipping on meals is normally 10–15 per cent at your discretion. Look out for *menús del día* (menus of the day) – sometimes simply called *menú*. These set menus include anything from one to four courses and usually a drink for an incredibly reasonable price.

Drink

No one should leave Peru without at least trying a Pisco Sour (*see p46*). The national drink is probably the country's most famous export and almost every Peruvian bar and restaurant can whip up this refreshing, but potent, cocktail. Peru is not normally associated with wine, but the districts around Pisco and Nazca have a rich wine-cultivating culture, and some of the better bottles are very drinkable. Peruvian *cervezas* (beers) are also perfectly tolerable – try Cusquena or Cristal. *Chica* (a corn-based spirit) is the drink of the Incas and still the drink of choice for many poor Peruvians.

Of Peru's *gaseosas* (fizzy soft drinks), the wonderfully named Inka Kola – luminous yellow and very sweet – is by far the most popular. There are some drinks that will never be seen outside Peru's borders; street sellers peddle *emoliente*, a kind of tea with herbs, and *chica morada* made with purple corn and sugar. As well as the freshly boiled version, *chica morada* can

also be bought in bottles and cans from shops.

Although Peru is a large producer of coffee, it is often hard to find a decent cup. Perhaps the best of the crop is swiped for the international market. *Mate de coca* (coca tea) is a pick-me-up, medicine and delicious tea. A proven cure for altitude sickness, it is used by the indigenous population to help them through their long days of hard work. The tea is made from the leaves of the coca plant (the raw ingredient of cocaine) but has none of the effects of the drug and is quite legal in Peru, although not in other countries.

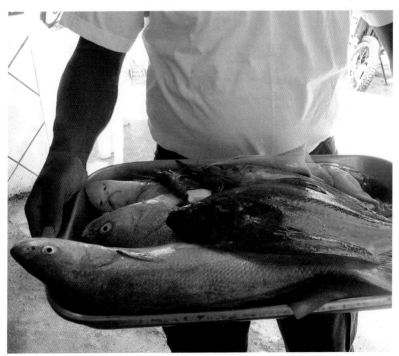

Opt for fish at lunchtime, when the catch is at its best

Entertainment

*During the day you are likely to be busy with sightseeing –
visiting museums and archaeological sites, wandering
around shops and haggling in the markets. Wherever you
go, expect to find Peruvians tuning in to technocumbia
and chicha, which fuse traditional Andean sounds with
modern Latin and dance beats. Combine dinner with
culture in one of the many restaurants offering live music
and folkloric shows, or hole up in a bar and test your
resistance to pisco, the nation's favourite tipple.*

High culture

Accomplished international performers
and orchestras have now put Lima on
their world tour itinerary. At news
kiosks, look for *El Comercio*, which has
daily listings. Since its own home
burned down, the National Symphony
Orchestra performs at the Museo de la
Nación (*see p32*). Dress up, as the locals
do, and take in a recital there, or enjoy

A carnival dancer in golden costume

a night at the opera at Teatro Segura (*see p165*).

Traditional folk music and dance

Lima attracts some of Andean folk music's biggest players, often performing in community centres and restaurants. Wealthy Arequipa is another hot spot, and Cusco is where most of the best artists head in peak season. The folk circuit revolves around clubs known as *peñas*, such as Sachún in Lima (*see p164*), which stages traditional dance ballets. The Brisas del Titicaca, which is always well attended, offers accomplished Andean song and dance, in an atmosphere that feels just a little touristy (*see p164*).

Late nights

In the provinces, a night out is a laid-back and low-key affair, but things do heat up in the major cities, such as Cusco and Lima. Nightclubs are a relatively new concept here, but late-night bars, where dancing is positively encouraged, abound. Licensing laws are loose, so places tend to close when the last person leaves. In Lima, try out one of the jazz bars that are popular with the (comparatively) rich middle classes. Nightclubs have sprung up in Barranco, San Isidro and Miraflores. Most are open from Thursday to Saturday until 3am. Many are members only, but show your passport, or make it clear you are a visitor, and you should have no problem getting in. At weekends, the beaches south of Lima attract the city's

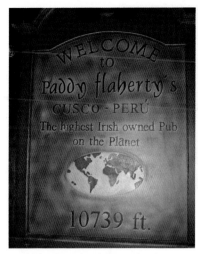

Cusco's bar scene is truly international

young pleasure-seekers and competent, if not internationally known, DJs. For starters, try La Huaka (*see p164*).

Más económico

Everyone likes to kick up their heels, but in Peru 50 per cent of people live below the poverty line, and have little or no cash to spend on entertainment, so leisure time means relaxing, chatting with friends and family, or an evening stroll around the plaza and park. Such pastimes are *más económico* (easier on the wallet), but are no less fun for that. A favourite spot with Limeños is El Parque Central in Miraflores. In the early afternoon, its open-air amphitheatre plays host to mime artists, theatre groups or dance ensembles (all for free), and, in the evenings, couples, families and friends wander and chat.

Shopping

Peru is a wonderful place to shop – from all-encompassing shopping malls with cinemas and restaurants to individual, friendly craft shops and colourful markets that are destinations in their own right (see p142). There are distinct regional variations, and sophisticated boutiques and malls are rarely found outside Lima. Cusco boasts artesanías *(craft shops) and arty galleries galore, but authentic food and clothes markets are found throughout the country.*

Capital purchases

Although there are many regional differences in terms of shopping opportunities, most items can be bought in Lima. As this is where most international travellers fly out from, it is sensible to make the bulk of your purchases here, either at the end of your trip or at the beginning (leave your purchases with a reputable hotel while you travel). Almost all shops are open until late in the evening, so shopping need not interrupt sightseeing. Avoid buying coca tea as a present, as it is illegal in many countries outside Peru.

Local handicrafts

Handicrafts from Peru make great souvenirs and gifts, and buying them supports traditional skills and small family businesses. Look out for pieces made of gold and silver, crafted using techniques handed down from Inca times, and local ceramics, often copies of pre-Columbian works of art. Musical instruments, such as drums and flutes, are another good buy. Jumpers made from alpaca are also popular. Puno is probably the best place to buy such goods, but watch out for cheap imitations as they may be synthetic. Weavings are another good purchase and integral to Peruvian culture. Every

Finger puppets for the kids

Traditional textiles and handmade jewellery on sale in Pisac market

village has its own distinct weaving patterns and traditions, some of which date back several thousand years.

Driving a hard bargain

Try to pay a fair price for any purchases, but also respect the rules of bargaining. Don't ask how much something costs if you have no intention of buying. When told a price, either agree or offer a lower amount (walking away at this stage is considered very rude). Give an amount that is considerably lower than you are prepared to pay. The law of bargaining means that you can never go below the first price you offer. If you get to an impasse, walking away will sometimes prompt the seller to relent and call you back to accept the last price offered.

FAIR TRADE

In some parts of Peru, traditional arts are dying out due to lack of demand, but visitors can make a positive impact. Buying fair-trade handicrafts not only benefits local communities but ultimately helps to safeguard aspects of the indigenous culture. In Cusco, the Center for Traditional Textiles (*Avenida Sol 603, next to Koricancha. www.incas.org*) preserves the 2,000-year tradition of Andean textiles. Visitors can see products being woven by hand and purchase fair-trade woollen goods and textiles. Peru Verde (*www.peruverde.org*) sells indigenous handicrafts in seven shops throughout Peru in order to generate income for Amazon communities.

Markets

From the hectic inner cities to the remote Amazon jungle, Peru's markets are its lifeblood. Much more than just shopping centres, they are places where goods are exchanged, important news is relayed, communities are strengthened and, of course, gossip is spread. For visitors, the markets are a window into everyday Peruvian life, and an atmospheric and rewarding experience. Even the shopping averse should visit a Peruvian market at least once on their trip.

Market day

If you are travelling around Peru for more than a week or two, you may actually get tired of eating in

Colours galore in the marketplace

restaurants. Local markets are a great source of fresh ingredients, and visiting one can be an experience in itself. A full picnic can be had for very little, and will often be the most delicious meal on your whole trip. In the country's omnipresent food markets, rudimentary Spanish can get you a long way, but, failing that, just smile and point.

The full range

Even the smallest market in Peru is colourful and vibrant, full of memorable sounds and smells. From the now touristy market in Pisac and workaday complexes in big cities such as Lima, to ramshackle beach and pavement stalls and goods arranged by the side of railway tracks, be prepared for a rich sensory overload.

Tours

Many tour agencies run trips to the more famous markets, such as the one in Pisac (see p64), but often the best way is to go on your own, or with a local who can describe the goods and give guidance about prices. For villagers, market day is a big social event – dressed in their 'Sunday best', they often combine it

It is market day every day in Peru

at your hotel, carry your money in a belt or bag inside clothing, and don't flaunt cameras or large amounts of cash. There will usually be plenty of good photo opportunities, but ask first before taking pictures of individuals.

Food

Fresh produce abounds. There are carts brimming with fruit and vegetables, mini mountains of nuts and grains, strung-up animal carcasses and sacks overspilling with rice. In the more traditional markets in the Andes, women can be seen carrying huge sacks of vegetables on their backs wrapped in brightly coloured shawls and laying their wares out on their textiles.

with attendance at church, and visits to family and friends. At the same time, of course, they shop for fresh ingredients, home wares and livestock. In tourist areas, the normal goods may be supplanted by crafts and clothes aimed at visitors. Those wanting to avoid the tourists at Pisac should head to nearby Chinchero, which is in an equally beautiful setting but is as yet undiscovered by most tourists (*see p124*).

Local life

Take time out from shopping to relax with a drink in a café or bar, and watch the market buzz. As well as livestock such as llamas and donkeys, and locals in their finery, you may catch a traditional performance of a local dance. In Pisac, *campesinos* (farm workers) from the surrounding villages gather at the Mercado de Treque (Barter Market). This is an ancient highland custom that dates to pre-Inca times in which locally grown goods, such as potatoes and corn, are exchanged for vital supplies of matches, salt and kerosene.

Common sense

In markets generally, there are bargains to be had, but in tourist areas the quality of products may be dubious. Be particularly wary about buying 'antiques'. Walk around first and then return to your favourite stalls. Take sensible precautions: leave valuables

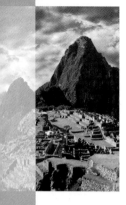

Sport and leisure

Although living at altitudes where most of us find it difficult to walk and breathe at the same time, the Peruvian people are incredibly active. In Lima, they live and breathe football, the nation's love. In the Andes, you will meet hikers and mountaineers whose stamina and agility will leave you speechless, and in the depths of the Colca Canyon the white-water rafting will have your heart beating like a drum. The area around Ica, south of Lima, is known for attracting sand boarders to its dunes.

Football

In 2004, Peru hosted the Copa América, the prestigious tournament where the nations of South and Central America compete in a three-week-long football frenzy. Brazil lifted the cup, but winning is no walk in the park in a continent where professional football is played almost the whole year round. Peru last won the Copa in 1975, led by free-scoring Teófilo Cubillas, considered the best Peruvian footballer of all time. Scotland fans will painfully recall the 1978 World Cup, when a team of Scottish stars, hyped to win the tournament, was summarily defeated 3–1 by the skilful Peruvians, with Cubillas scoring twice.

Peruvians are, of course, football crazy. Look even mildly interested, and you are likely to be invited to join a kick-around in the streets. In remote areas, games between villages are celebratory cacophonic affairs. Like everywhere, football is the people's game, played by everyone, including the poor and dispossessed, often on waste ground without shoes, and sometimes without a real ball. Visitors are encouraged to pack two or three (deflated) footballs as presents for schools, and for orphanages – of which there are many in Peru, thanks to the effects of earthquakes and years of civil war.

Traditionally, the national league has been dominated by two Lima teams – Alianza Lima and Universitario de Deportes. Newcomer Sporting Cristal has made inroads into this hegemony, largely because they are backed by a large brewery and take a more serious approach to the 'business of football'. If your timing is right, a game between Alianza and Universitario at the latter's Estadio Monumental 'U' is a treat. With a capacity of 80,000 and plans afoot to increase it to 96,500, the 'U' is South America's second-largest football stadium, and, on derby day, perhaps its noisiest (*see p165*).

Hiking

Peru's archaeological and natural riches can best be appreciated by hiking the same routes that the ancients did, whether it's down into the depths of the Colca Canyon, along the Inca Trail to Machu Picchu, or 'touching the void' in the central Andes (*see p123*).

One of hiking's golden rules is 'be prepared' (the other is 'leave nothing but footprints, take nothing but photographs'). Plan your trip carefully, allowing plenty of time for acclimatisation above 3,000m (10,000ft). Bring the right equipment (*see p146*) and be sure to choose an experienced guide. Book through a reputable company, and listen to advice from the experienced hikers you meet in the mountain towns. Ensure a reliable person knows when you should be back, and always register when entering national parks.

Horse-riding

If you're an enthusiast, or even if it's your first time, Peru is a great place to get in the saddle. Prices are low, the scenery is stunning, and riding through those mountain passes is a picnic

Sand boarders on their way to slide down a dune near Ica

compared with hiking them. From Huaraz, it's possible to organise riding trips into the Huascarán National Park on a four- or five-day tour, or you can opt to ride your way through the

---

HIKING EQUIPMENT

Below is a basic list of equipment required for hiking tours, although on many tours (for example, the Inca Trail) guides can be employed to carry your equipment.

All hiking tours
Backpack
Basic first-aid kit and personal medicines
Binoculars
Camera
Copy of insurance documents
Flashlight and headlight
Hiking boots
Immunisation certificates
Insect repellent
Passport
Personal item kit (toothbrush, etc.)
Sunglasses
Water bottle or Camelbak
Additional layers/waterproofs

Additional for multi-day hiking tours
1 pair warm gloves
2 pairs zip-off hiking shorts/trousers
3–4 shirts
4 pairs hiking socks
Biodegradable soap for clothes and hair
Clean clothing and shoes for restaurants, etc.
Facecloth and small towel
Rain jacket, hat and trousers
Sleeping bag
Small day pack for your camera
Sun hat
Tent
Thermarest sleeping mat with pillow
Warm hat
Warm insulated jacket
Warm sweater/fleece

Sacred Valley near Cusco, taking in such treasures as Ollantaytambo on the way.

Mountain biking

Growing in popularity, mountain bikes are easy to rent all over Peru. April to December is the best time for mountain biking around Pachamac and the hills south of Lima. The Paracas Peninsula is another popular spot, with its craggy coast and dunes. For those with good lung capacity, there is the Cordillera Blanca, where there are scores of tough trails, with altitude climbs followed by exhilarating descents. The route from Lagunas Llanganuco (3,800m/12,468ft) to Yungay is popular, as is the more challenging Punta Olímpica (4,800m/15,749ft) route. Both of these are best cycled between May and October. Always travel in a group and with a reputable company.

Mountaineering

The same general advice as given in the 'Hiking' section (see p145) applies here. However, obviously the Andean mountain range is not to be taken lightly, and only experienced climbers should be tempted to ascend to any summits here. For beginners who want a thorough grounding in camp craft and basic mountaineering skills, the Skyline Adventure School (tel: (043) 427 097; www.sladventureschool.com) offers a variety of courses out of Huaraz into the Cordillera Blanca (see p50).

Rafting

Rafters should be cautious of Peru's fast-moving and dangerous rivers – people have been killed while rafting here. When gauging conditions, don't rely solely on those that have a commercial interest – check with local authorities and do your research first. Leave a detailed timetable with a friend and with the authorities before you depart, and go with an experienced, reputable outfit. Obey the instructions of the guides and boat captains and never take to the water without your helmet and life jacket. For a list of rafting destinations (the best of which are probably the Colca and Cotahuasi rivers), visit *www.peru.info*

Climbing the Ranrapalca peak in the Cordillera Blanca

Children

Peruvians are likely to make you feel very much at home as a family, and locals will, quite literally, welcome your children with open arms – whether they are sitting down to dinner, enduring a long bus ride or playing in the park. Although Peru may not be an obvious destination for children, there is plenty to keep youngsters busily amused, and the countryside is a natural playground.

Lima

Peru's capital is not necessarily appealing to children, but in fact there is plenty for children to do here. Larcomar Mall (*www.larcomar.com*) has bowling, games machines and cinema screens showing films in English. You will probably want to avoid Huachipa Zoo, which does not keep animals in the best conditions; instead stick to Parque de las Leyendas (*Avenida La Marina*) with its zoo, gardens and playground.

Nazca

A ride in a small plane over the Nazca Lines is a guaranteed thrill for children. Show them the hummingbird, monkey and spaceman drawn in the desert, and then take the children to the nearby Cementerio de Chauchilla with its spooky graves, complete with mummies (*see p45*).

Cusco and Machu Picchu

The walk to Machu Picchu will be too much for most children, but youngsters will love the train ride, looking for llamas and hearing tales of high priests and sacrificial victims. In Cusco, point out the giant zigzagging walls that were made to look like puma teeth, and take your children to the Rodadero in Sacsayhuamán, a polished rock face that they can slide down.

Arequipa

Introduce your offspring to Juanita, a frozen 14-year-old Inca girl who was sacrificed over 500 years ago on Mount Ampato. Discovered only in 1995, this young girl is housed in the city's Museo Santuarios Andinos (*see p81*).

Lake Titicaca

Recount some of the legends about the freezing waters where the Inca sun god gave birth to Manco Cápac and his sister Mama Ocllo. The shape of Lake Titicaca is said to be like a giant puma that is opening its mouth to

Seeing how Peruvian children live can be a lesson to us all

eat the 'rabbit' of Puno Bay. Boat rides to the floating islands are great fun, where children can watch the local Uros people making reed boats with striking animal heads. In Puno, Parque Huajsapata (Huajsapata Park) has an enormous white statue of Manco Cápac and some wonderful natural rock slides.

The Amazon

The jungle offers young visitors the chance to play Tarzan high in the rainforest canopy (*see p106*), and to see exotic animals while charging along in a river boat.

The north coast

Farms here allow visitors to see, and even ride, the famous Paso Fino horses. At Chán Chán, children can climb the platforms or play hide and seek, while parents explore the important archaeological ruins.

STREET CHILDREN

In Peru, seeing children working and begging on the street can be a powerful experience for adults and children alike. More than a quarter of children here do not receive any education, but organisations such as SOS Children's Villages (*www.soschildrensvillages.org.uk*) educate street children and have programmes that allow you to sponsor a Peruvian child.

Essentials

Arriving

The approximate flight time to Lima is 15 hours from London (via Madrid), 9 hours from New York, 6 hours from Los Angeles, 5 hours from Miami, 20 hours from Sydney via Santiago or 25 hours via Los Angeles.

From Australia and New Zealand

Qantas flies from Sydney and Auckland to Santiago in Chile. From there, connect with LAN Peru to Lima. Alternatively, fly from Auckland, Sydney, Melbourne or Brisbane to Los Angeles (Qantas and other air carriers fly this route), and connect from there.

From Europe

Travellers from Europe may prefer to avoid passing through the USA, where you must disembark and clear your luggage through customs. US carriers in general are prone to delays and cancellations. There are no direct flights to Lima from London, so a transfer at Madrid is another option. From Madrid, Iberia flies direct, and Avianca connects in Bogotá; both are good options. From Frankfurt, LAN Peru flies via Santiago in Chile. From Amsterdam, KLM flies direct to Lima.

Travellers from the UK should compare budget airlines to European hubs, with onward scheduled flights, against the price of flying all the way with one airline. For complex itineraries and good deals, try a specialist travel company such as Journey Latin America (*www.journeylatinamerica.co.uk*) or Trailfinders (*www.trailfinders.com*).

From North America

Lima's international Jorge Chávez airport (code LIM) is where most visitors touch down. US carriers to Peru include American Airlines, Continental and Delta via hubs such as Atlanta, Dallas, Houston, Los Angeles and Miami. LAN Peru flies direct from New York, and Air Canada from Toronto.

From South Africa

South African Airways flies from Johannesburg to Lima via São Paulo in Brazil. Alternatively, fly via the USA (*see above*).

AIRLINE WEBSITES

Air Canada	*www.aircanada.com*
Air New Zealand	*www.airnewzealand.com*
American Airlines	*www.aa.com*
Avianca	*www.avianca.com*
Continental	*www.continental.com*
Delta	*www.delta.com*
Iberia	*www.iberia.com*
KLM	*www.klm.com*
LAN Peru	*www.lan.com*
Qantas	*www.qantas.com*
South African Airways	*www.flysaa.com*

Customs

Entering Peru

The following items are exempt from duty upon entry to Peru:

- 3 litres ($5^1/_4$ pints) of alcohol, 400 cigarettes (20 packs) or 50 cigars
- Gifts to the value of US$300, with no individual item worth more than US$100
- Personal equipment, such as mountain bikes and tents
- New items for personal use, including cameras, laptops and mobile phones

If you are bringing in new items (perhaps purchased duty-free on the way over) then discard the packaging and put them in your luggage, wherever possible. Otherwise, customs officials might assess them for duty allowances, and you will be required to provide a bond or letter of guarantee to prevent you selling the goods in the country.

Leaving Peru

In markets, be wary of jewellery or trinkets that look as if they may be made from a plant or animal species. Bird feathers, insects and plant seeds of endangered species are often used, illegally, to make handicrafts. Buying such items endangers biodiversity, and the export of them is obviously forbidden. Also prohibited is the export of archaeological items and antiquities dating from the pre-Columbian and

A plane at Nazca that takes visitors to see the mysterious Nazca Lines

colonial eras – even fragments. Plenty of reproduction items are, of course, on sale, and export should be no problem, provided you can show evidence of their origin. Get a certificate from the National Institute of Culture, which protects Peru's heritage – it has offices in all major cities and a kiosk at Lima's international airport.

Departing

From the centre of Lima, the airport is a half-hour drive, but perhaps twice as long in rush hour. Expect to pay a small departure tax at the airport (children under two years of age are exempt). Payment must be paid in cash before boarding.

Electricity

Domestic power supply is 220 volts AC, 60Hz – twin flat and twin round plugs are both standard here. European adaptors will not work, so bring a world travel adaptor.

Money

The local currency is the neuvo sol, divided into 100 céntimos, but US dollars are widely accepted too. Bring your debit card – they are the cheapest way to get local currency – and a couple of different credit cards. Visa is the most widely accepted credit card. When making purchases, the retailer may sometimes need to obtain telephone confirmation. If this doesn't happen, your card may be frozen until you telephone your bank, so it's good to have a backup. Some shops require sight of your driver's licence, passport or other ID. In remote villages, you might get a bad exchange rate for traveller's cheques; always try to exchange them in major cities whenever possible.

Opening hours

Many shops are open all day from around 10am until 7pm, but opening hours vary from place to place, and may change unexpectedly.

Passports and visas

Tourists from Australia, Canada, New Zealand, South Africa, the UK and the USA do not require a visa to enter the country. For visa requirements from all other countries refer to *www.peruvianembassy.us*. All visitors must have a passport valid for at least six months from the date they enter the country. On arrival, your passport will be stamped valid for a 90-day stay, and you will be given a tourist card that must be retained until departure.

Foreigners are legally required to carry their passports with them at all times, but a photocopy is safer and usually sufficient.

Pharmacies and minor ailments

Common medicines, such as antibiotics, can be bought in *farmacias* or *boticas* (chemists/drugstores) quite cheaply and without restrictions. However, make sure medicines have not expired.

Pharmacists are generally helpful and can be consulted for illnesses considered too minor for a doctor.

Post

The postal service is slow. Lima's main post office, the Correo Central, is just off the main plaza. Larger hotels will send your postcards. Anything important should be sent with DHL, UPS or FedEx.

Public holidays

1 January – New Year's Day
March/April – Maundy Thursday
March/April – Good Friday
1 May – Labour Day
29 June – St Peter and St Paul's Day
28–29 July – Independence Day
30 August – St Rosa of Lima Day
8 October – Battle of Angamos
1 November – All Saints' Day
8 December – Immaculate Conception
25 December – Christmas Day

Suggested reading
For adults

Bel Canto by Ann Patchett (2001)
Set in an unnamed South American country that is almost certainly Peru, this award-winning political novel is a wonderful work of magical realism.
The Bridge of San Luis Rey by Thornton Wilder (1927)
'On Friday noon, July the twentieth, 1714, the finest bridge in all Peru broke and precipitated five travelers into the gulf below...' is the first sentence of this short, slick Pulitzer Prize winner.

Death in the Andes by Mario Vargas Llosa (1997)
Part thriller, part political treatise on Peruvian politics and the Shining Path, by one of the greatest Latin American writers.
Eight Feet in the Andes. Travels with a Mule in Unknown Peru by Dervla Murphy (2003)
The insightful story of an acclaimed yet unassuming author, her nine-year-old daughter and a mule called Juana, who together make a brave trip across the Andes.
Inca Gold by Clive Cussler (1994)
This book features hero Dirk Pitt – an adventurer in the Indiana Jones mould. In this fast-moving romp through the Andes, he is on an Inca treasure hunt that leads him to shipwrecks, jungles and ancient ruins.
Machu Picchu by Pablo Neruda and Barry Brukoff (2001)
A beautiful book that captures the spirit of Machu Picchu by combining Chilean poet Neruda's evocative poem *The Heights of Machu Picchu* with Brukoff's magical photographs.
Touching the Void by Joe Simpson (1997)
A remarkable tale of surviving a fall from the Andean peak Siula Grande.
The White Rock: An Exploration of the Inca Heartland by Hugh Thomson (2003)
A world expert on Peru imaginatively recreates the Inca domain after 20 years of solid research. This authoritative work is a joy.

An unusual way to get around Chivay, near the Colca Canyon

For children

A Bear Called Paddington by Michael Bond and Peggy Fortnum (2001) The first in the series of illustrated books about the bear from 'deepest darkest Peru' continues to delight adults and children nearly 50 years on.

The Incredible Incas by Terry Deary (2000) Gruesome tales of child and guinea-pig sacrifices and jewellery made of llama toenails from the deservedly acclaimed *Horrible Histories* series. By the same author, the *Incredible Incas Activity Book* (2005) has conquistadors as cartoon characters and an Inca initiation game.

Tax

Goods and services, including hotel and restaurant bills, are subject to a general sales tax (IGV) of around 19 per cent, although the amount changes from time to time. However, a tour package purchased outside Peru is exempt from IGV. Peru is not currently part of the Global Refund tax-free shopping scheme, so tax on large purchases cannot be claimed back at the airport.

REGIONAL TELEPHONE CODES

Arequipa *054*
Cusco *084*
Huaraz *043*
Iquitos *065*
Lima *01*
Machu Picchu (Aguas Calientes) *084*
Nazca *056*
Puno *051*

Telephones

If you bring your own mobile, it should be GSM1900 capable. With such phones (not network locked), visitors can buy a cheap prepaid SIM card for calls within Peru. This will be useful if your itinerary is flexible and you need to make arrangements as you go. Using your own SIM card to make or receive calls will be very expensive.

For calls home, it is cheaper to buy an international telephone card, or to use an internet phone (for example, SKYPE) in a web café.

When dialling Peru from overseas, use your country's international access code followed by Peru's country code (*51*), followed by the regional code (*see below left*) without the zero at the beginning, followed by the telephone number. For example, a hotel in Cusco may be listed as *235 643*.
From the UK, dial *(00 51 84) 235 643*.
From Lima, dial *(084) 235 643*.
In Cusco, dial *235 643*.

Internet and email

Internet cafés are pretty common in cities and tourist areas, but less so off the beaten track. Smart hotels and many backpackers' hostels have fast internet connections.

If you wish to type the @ sign (in Spanish, *arroba*) on the keyboard, hold down ALT then press 6, then 4. If that doesn't work, ask one of the locals.

Time differences

In general, allow plenty of time for everything – there is sometimes a bit of bureaucracy to deal with, downpours can slow you down, and in the summer it is too hot to move quickly.

In terms of time difference, Peru is five hours behind London, or six hours in British Summer Time (BST). Other time differences are listed below.

Auckland	+17 (+18 Eastern Standard Time – EST)
Cape Town	+7
London	+5 (+6 BST)
Los Angeles	−3 (−2 Pacific Daylight Time – PDT)
New York	+0 (+1 Eastern Daylight Time – EDT)
Sydney	+15 (+16 EST)
Toronto	+0 (+1 EDT)

Toilets

Toilet doors are marked with 'baño', 'S.H' or 'SS.HH'. The latter two are abbreviations for *servicio higienico*, which is the rather formal expression. Expect to pay no more than 20 céntimos at public toilets. To prevent blockages, used toilet paper should be thrown not into the toilet, but into the adjacent basket. Be wary of unhygienic facilities (*see p160*).

Travellers with disabilities

Regrettably, facilities for those with disabilities are poor in many regions of the country, and even in the big cities. However, things are changing, and there is a wealth of information on the web so that travellers can plan their trip. Start with *www.access-able.com.* If you decide against a hotel because of poor access, let them know so that things may improve in future.

Websites

www.andeantravelweb.com
Over 500 pages of useful and up-to-date travel information provided by a non-profit organisation that promotes Peru and runs community projects.
www.enjoyperu.com
This travel agency site features an online magazine with interesting, well-researched articles on a range of subjects relating to Peru.
www.expatperu.com
Although aimed primarily at the expat community, this is a useful site for event listings, travel forums and links.
www.incasdelperu.com
Incas del Peru is an agency and learning centre based in Huancayo that focuses on Peru's people and culture. Its website gives details of trips, volunteer opportunities, and courses that include music, weaving and Quechua.
www.peru.info
The national tourist office site is a comprehensive resource for planning a trip. Its excellent searchable directory includes bus companies, tour agencies and accommodation listed under regions. The site also has contact details and opening times for tourist offices

around the country, and it offers a free 24-hour telephone service (*(01) 574 8000*) and a complaints procedure if something goes wrong with a tour agency or airline.

www.rumbosperu.com
A quirky online illustrated magazine featuring articles on subjects such as archaeology, art and adventure, along with an online shop and gallery.

www.saexplorers.org
The South American Explorers Club promotes awareness of the continent and cross-cultural interaction. The site allows members (a fee is charged) to access its enormously useful resources and purchase invaluable information packs on subjects ranging from trip reports to volunteer opportunities.

The evocative train ride from Cusco to Machu Picchu

Language

It may be a cliché, but a little of the local language will go a long way in Peru. Spanish, which is spoken rather differently than in Spain, is one of the two official languages. The other is Quechua, the language of the Incas. The Spanish did all they could to wipe Quechua out, but it is still spoken by 10 million people throughout South America, and mostly by the rural population in Peru. 'Llama', 'potato', 'gaucho' and 'puma' are just some of the Quechua words that have entered the English language. Aymara is also spoken, but it is not considered an official language.

SPANISH

GENERAL VOCABULARY

English	Spanish	Pronunciation
Yes	Sí	*see*
No	No	*no*
Please	Por favor	*por faVOR*
Thank you (very much)	(Muchas) gracias	*(MOOchaahs) GRAsiyas*
You're welcome	De nada	*de NAda*
Hello	Hola	*ola*
Goodbye	Adiós	*adeeYOS*
Good morning/day	Buenos días	*BWEnos DEEyas*
Good afternoon/evening	Buenas tardes	*BWEnas TARdes*
Good evening (after dark)	Buenas noches	*BWEnas NOches*
Excuse me (to get attention)	Disculpe	*desKOOLpe*
Excuse me (to apologise)	Perdón	*perDON*
Sorry	Lo siento	*lo sYENto*
Help!	¡Socorro!	*SOHcohro*
Today	Hoy	*oy*
Tomorrow	Mañana	*manYAna*
Yesterday	Ayer	*aYER*
Where?	¿Dónde?	*donde*
When?	¿Cuándo?	*KWANdo*
Why?	¿Porque?	*porKE*
How?	¿Cómo?	*Como*

USEFUL WORDS AND PHRASES

English	Spanish	Pronunciation
How much is it?	¿Cuánto es?	*KWANto es*
Expensive	Caro/a	*KAROla*
I don't understand	No entiendo	*no entYENdoe*
Do you speak English?	¿Habla Usted Ingles?	*ablah OOsted eenGLES*
My name is...	Me llamo...	*meh YAmoh...*

www.bbc.co.uk/languages/spanish/quickfix allows you to download phrases in Spanish as an MP3, and you can listen to them being spoken when you click on them.

QUECHUA

GENERAL VOCABULARY

English	Quechua (pronounce as it is written)
Yes	Arí
No	Mana
Please	Allichu
Thank you	Añay
Hello	Allillanchu
Goodbye	Rikunakusun or Wuasleglla

USEFUL WORDS AND PHRASES

English	Quechua
How are you?	Ima hinalla?
Where are you from?	Maymantataq hamunki?
I don't understand	Mana jhapikkana
My name is...	Ñuqap ... sutiymi

www.quechua.org.uk is a comprehensive website with historical and linguistic facts about Quechua, including sound recordings and information about spelling and grammar.

www.travlang.com/languages lists some basic words and phrases in Quechua that can be clicked on to hear them being spoken.

Emergencies

Emergency numbers

Police: *105*
Fire: *116*
Emergency medical attention: *117*
Ambulance (private): *(01) 225 4040*

Tourist police

Arequipa: *(054) 251 270/239 888*
Cusco: *(084) 249 654*
Lima North: *(01) 424 2053*
Lima South: *(01) 460 4525*

The SPT (Tourist Protection Service) was set up to help tourists who have consumer problems (for example, with hotels or shops). For petty crime, your first stop should be the tourist police, but calling the SPT is a good backup.
SPT (Tourist Protection Service): *(01) 224 7888*

Health care

Ensure that you have adequate health-care insurance before you leave for Peru. Look out for cheap deals on the internet, but check carefully what is covered, particularly if you are planning adventure activities, or are visiting the Amazon. Your policy should include cover for international medical evacuation by air ambulance. Inform your insurer of any pre-existing medical condition before obtaining a quote. You may find that annual cover costs little more than single-trip policies and is well worth investigating.

Vaccinations should be arranged at least two months before you travel. Some or all of the following are recommended, depending on which parts of the country you will be visiting: polio, tetanus, typhoid, yellow fever, hepatitis A and rabies. Carry your vaccination card with you in Peru.

For the jungle, ask your doctor in advance about anti-malarial courses. If you catch it, there are clinics in Iquitos, Puerto Maldonado and other jungle towns.

Be wary of getting too much sun – wear high-factor sun cream, sunglasses and a light-coloured hat. Even on cloudy days, sunburn and heatstroke are prevalent.

Bacterial diarrhoea, if it strikes, will usually clear up within a week, but to avoid severe dehydration consume plenty of electrolytic (rehydrating) drinks – you can get soluble powders in almost every pharmacy. If you run out, drink dissolved sugar and salt in water. If symptoms persist for more than a week, treat with antibiotics. In mountainous regions, watch out for altitude sickness (*see p51*).

If you take prescription medication, or in case you need new glasses or contact lenses, hold on to your original prescription and a photocopy. Women who use tampons should bring them

Toilets are often quite primitive and sometimes really dirty. It's a good idea to bring your own paper with you, as what you find in toilets here is often rough, usually single-ply, and, more often than not, nonexistent. You are advised to drink bottled rather than tap water.

Safety and crime
Drugs

If you are offered drugs, be very careful. It is illegal even to 'consider to perhaps accept' an offer to buy some. You could potentially be walking into a police trap, and face a stiff sentence. Occasionally, you may be told (even by a police officer) that it is acceptable to hold a small amount of marijuana. Again, be wary.

Money scams

Watch out for false banknotes, particularly when receiving change for large notes. Rather than hand over a large note for a small purchase, show your note first and ask whether the seller has change (*¿Tienes cambio?*). A common ruse is to take your note, switch it, then hand it back saying it cannot be changed. Don't be shy about checking banknotes – locals do it as a matter of course.

Muggings

In cities, stay alert; avoid unlit or unpopulated areas, especially if you are alone at night. Petty crime can occasionally turn violent. A dirty old

Start taking anti-malarial drugs before travelling to the Amazon

from home – they are not widely available outside Lima.

Electrically heated showers are common, but the water heater is commonly situated at the shower head. Check it before you turn on the shower, especially if you are tall, since touching unprotected or badly installed cables can result in a nasty electric shock. In the Andean region, where water is often heated only by solar energy, the temperature of the hot water supply can vary with the weather and time of day. In cheap hostels, hot water can run out at busy times of the day.

backpack containing an expensive camera is safer than a new backpack with just your dirty socks in it. Consider dispersing your money around different pockets, rather than carrying a full wallet, or use a concealed money belt.

Police

Tourist police are a separate organisation from the normal police force: dressed in white shirts rather than the usual police green ones, they can generally speak English and are quite helpful to tourists. Avoid getting into an argument with the police, as they are then less likely to help – a charm offensive is best.

Dealing with the police can take time. To get a copy of a police report for insurance purposes, you must go to a branch of Banco de la Nación and pay 3 soles. If you don't do this, the police won't give you a copy of the report, and obviously you can arrange this only during working hours.

Embassies and consulates

If you get into trouble with the police, have an accident, lose your passport or become a victim of crime, you may need to contact your embassy or consulate, so check you have their details before your visit. If you're planning a lengthy stay, it's also a good idea to register with them.

Australian Consulate
Avenida Victor Andres Belaunde 147,
Via Principal 155, Torre Real Tres,
Office 1301, San Isidro, Lima.
Tel: (01) 222 8281.
Fax: (01) 221 4996.
www.dfat.gov.au

British Embassy
Torre Parque Mar (Piso 22), Avenida José Larco, 1301, Miraflores, Lima.
Tel: (01) 617 3000.
Fax: (01) 617 3100.
www.ukinperu.fco.gov.uk

Canadian Embassy
Calle Bolognesi 228, Miraflores, Lima.
Tel: (01) 319 3200.
http://geo.international.gc.ca/
latin-america/peru

New Zealand Consulate
Los Nogales 510 (Piso 3), San Isidro, Lima.
Tel: (01) 422 7491. Fax: (01) 422 2999.

South African Embassy
Avenida Victor Andres Belaunde 147, Torre Real Tres, Office 801, San Isidro, Lima. Tel: (01) 440 9996.
Fax: (01) 422 3881.
www.dfa.gov.za

US Embassy
Avenida La Encalada, Cuadra 17, Monterrico, Lima. Tel: (01) 434 3000.
Fax: (01) 618 2724.
http://lima.usembassy.gov

Some of the aforementioned countries also have consulates in other major cities. See their websites for more details. Finally, it's always a good idea to check your government's advice before you travel.

Directory

Accommodation price guide

A scale of one to four stars has been used as a price guide, with one star indicating the cheapest option and four stars the most expensive. Price bands are based on the average cost of a double room with two people sharing. Breakfast will probably be included in the top two bands, but not in the bottom two. Often an additional bed can be added to a room for a fraction of the total. Before you book, be sure to find out whether credit cards are accepted if you are short on cash.

★	up to 90 soles
★★	90–180 soles
★★★	180–350 soles
★★★★	over 350 soles

Eating out price guide

The star system opposite is based on the average price of a meal for one person without drinks or tips.

★	up to 20 soles
★★	20–40 soles
★★★	40–70 soles
★★★★	over 70 soles

Addresses may be given without a street number such as 'Morales esq. Gamarra'. In such cases, 'esq.' is short for *esquina* (corner), so go to the first street where the second street crosses it.

LIMA, NAZCA AND THE SOUTH COAST

Lima

ACCOMMODATION

Hostal Mami Panchita ★
A Peruvian- and Dutch-run guesthouse that is both friendly and clean. It is conveniently situated between the centre, Miraflores and the airport.
Avenida Federico Gallesi 198, San Miguel.
Tel: (01) 263 7203.
www.mamipanchita.com

Suites Antique ★★★
The location 20 minutes from the airport makes this accommodation convenient for those making a stopover. Families in particular will appreciate the rooms, which all have kitchenettes and a lounge.
Avenida 2 de Mayo 954, San Isidro.
Tel: (01) 222 1094.
www.suitesantique.com

Country Club Lima Hotel ★★★★
A five-star hotel with all facilities, built in 1927. As well as art from the Museo de Osma, guests can enjoy afternoon tea, a traditional English bar, a fitness centre, an outdoor swimming pool and use of the 18-hole, par-72 golf course.
Los Eucaliptos 590, San Isidro.
Tel: (01) 611 9000.
www.hotelcountry.com

Eating Out

Café Café ★

Go for tasty sandwiches and great coffee served in a faintly bohemian atmosphere surrounded by locals. There are branches in other locations in the city.
Martin Olaya 250, Miraflores. Open: until the early hours.

Las Brujas de Cachiche ★★★

There may be better-value lunch buffets in the city, but this one cannot be beaten for spectacular modern Peruvian food and great service. Open for dinner too. Reservations essential.
Calle Bolognesi 472, Miraflores. Tel: (01) 447 1133. www. brujasdecachiche.com.pe

Manos Morenas ★★★

Tuck into duck (*pato*), just one of the *criolla* specialities served up in this elegant, 100-year-old mansion with a pretty patio. Manos Morenas translates as 'Black Hands', after the creative force behind Afro-Peruvian cuisine.
Avenida Pedro de Osma 409, Barranco.

Tel: (01) 467 0421. www. manosmorenasperu.com

La Rosa Nautica ★★★★

Try to visit one of the city's most beautiful restaurants at sunset to enjoy the view from its pier location. Appropriately enough, seafood is the speciality, with good-value set meals.
Espigón 4, Costa Verde, Miraflores. Tel: (01) 447 0057. www.larosanautica.com

Entertainment

Asociación Internacional Jazz Perú

The sounds of traditional jazz music, with some Afro-Peruvian influences, fill the air in this venue. On Monday and Tuesday, jam sessions welcome singers and instrumentalists who can just drop by.
Avenida Benavides 414. Tel: (01) 720 6186. www.jazzperu.org

Brisas del Titicaca

Don't expect to see many locals here. Go instead for lively music and dance from Wednesday to Saturday. Reservations can be made on the website, which carries full details of events.

Jirón Wakulski 168. Tel: (01) 332 1901/ 332 1881. www.brisasdeltiticaca.com

La Huaka Beach Club

This nightclub on the beach hosts popular, Peruvian and occasionally international DJs. Saturday is the big night. No dress code.
Km 97.5, Panamericana Sur. Tel: (01) 224 7878. www.lahuaka.com (Spanish only).

Jazz Zone

A variety of jazz is on the menu at this relaxing, well-established spot.
Avenida La Paz 656, Pasaje El Suche, Miraflores. Tel: (01) 241 8139. www.jazzzoneperu.com

Sachún

Enjoy live folk music and traditional dance ballet while having dinner. Call ahead to make a reservation.
Avenida del Ejército 657. Tel: (01) 441 0123. www.sachunperu.com. Closed: Mon.

Symphony Orchestra

This highly regarded company performs recitals throughout

the year to packed audiences.
Museo de la Nación, Avenida Javier Prado. Tel: (01) 476 9875.
Teatro Segura
A variety of musical concerts and excellent opera is performed here.
Huancavelica 265. Tel: (01) 426 7206.

SPORT AND LEISURE
Club Universitario de Deportes
Match tickets are available on the door of this great stadium, or can be arranged with larger hotels to include a guide and transport.
Estadio Teodoro Fernández (Monumental 'U'). www. universitariodeportes.biz (Spanish only).

Nazca
ACCOMMODATION
Hotel Alegría ★★
A good-value budget option with a small pool, restaurant and internet access. Ask for one of the rooms with air conditioning. A reputable tour agency is attached.
Calle Lima 168. Tel: (056) 522 702. www.hotelalegria.net

Hotel Nazca Lines ★★★
The cool white colonnades, courtyard and swimming pool provide a little oasis in this dusty desert town, although service and décor may disappoint. A bonus is the planetarium in the grounds (*admission charge*).
Jirón Bolognesi, Nazca. Tel: (056) 522 293.

EATING OUT
Hotel Cantayo restaurant ★★★
Reliable cuisine from a formal restaurant that is part of the Hotel Cantayo spa and resort complex just out of town. Enjoy Peruvian and international cuisine, but expect to be surrounded by tour groups.
Puquio Kms 3–4. Tel: (056) 522 264. www.hotelcantayo.com

ENTERTAINMENT
Hotel Cantayo
Take it easy with a massage, whirlpool, sauna and maybe even a little yoga in this 'relaxation resort'. But avoid the much talked-about garden of exotic animals

as it includes caged and chained animals.
Hotel Cantayo, Puquio Kms 3–4. Tel: (056) 522 264. www.hotelcantayo.com

Paracas Peninsula
SPORT AND LEISURE
Peru Adventure Tours
This reputable company offers mountain-biking tours around the peninsula to see the spectacular cliff formations and rich wildlife, as well as the chance to hurtle down the vertiginous dunes.
Calle Jerusalén At 410–A, Arequipa. Tel: (054) 221 658. www. peruadventuretours.com

THE CENTRAL ANDES
Cordillera Blanca
ACCOMMODATION
Hostal Churup ★★
A popular, light and airy place, where the knowledgeable owners are invaluable when it comes to planning your trip into the mountains. Included in your stay is a free one-day hike. Dorms and private en-suite rooms available.

*Jirón Amadeo Figueroa
1257, La Soldedad,
Huaraz.
Tel: (043) 424 200.
www.churup.com*

Hotel Colomba ★★

A charming old hacienda
set in well-tended
gardens about 15
minutes from the main
square. Bungalows and
private rooms are
available, and there is a
gym, games room and
several computers with
internet access.

*Jirón Francisco de Zela
210, Huaraz.
Tel: (043) 421 501.
www.huarazhotel.com*

Andino Club Hotel ★★★

A peach of a hotel with
a sauna and 60 well-
appointed rooms. All
have internet access, and
some have balconies
and fireplaces.

*Pedro Cochachin
357, Huaraz.
Tel: (043) 421 662.
www.hotelandino.com*

EATING OUT

Bistro de Los Andes ★

French-Peruvian fusion
place that is great for
vegetarians and meat
eaters alike. If you arrive
on the night bus from

Lima, pop in as it opens
for breakfast from 5am.

*Julio de Morales
823, Huaraz.
Tel: (043) 726 249.*

Siam de Los Andes ★★

Stir-fry, curry and Thai
specialities are the order
of the day in this superb
eatery run by Naresuan,
a native of Thailand who
has trained his staff to
perfection. Try for a
table near the fire to
avoid draughts.

*Julio de Morales esq.
Gamarra, Huaraz.
Tel: (043) 509 173.*

Chalet Suisse ★★★

Pricey, but relaxed,
with an accomplished
fondue and steak menu.
Attached to the Andino
Club Hotel, it has great
views, but can get busy
in peak season.

*Pedro Cochachin
357, Huaraz.
Tel: (043) 421 662.*

ENTERTAINMENT

Café Andino

Good coffee hang-out
with a book exchange,
music and board games.

*Jirón 28 de Julio 562,
Huaraz.*

Las Kenas

Very popular, this disco

sometimes has popular
live Andean music
performances.

*Jirón Gabino Uribe 620
(off Luzuriaga), Huaraz.*

El Tambo

The late-night place to
find other travellers,
exchange stories and
dance with the locals,
especially at weekends.
You may be asked for a
cover charge.

*José de la Mar 776, three
blocks from Luzuriaga,
Huaraz.*

SPORT AND LEISURE

Explorandes

Long-established outfit
with reliable guides and
solid environmental
credentials. Explorandes
can arrange hiking and
mountain-bike tours,
and will give you help
with equipment hire.
There are offices in Lima
and Cusco too.

*Avenida Centenario
489, Huaraz.
Tel: (043) 721 960.
www.explorandes.com*

**Peruvian Andes
Adventures**

A professional company
offering day walks, longer
treks, climbing and a
range of activities.

It also operates in the Cordillera Huayhuash.
Jirón José Olaya 532, Huaraz.
Tel: (043) 721 864.
www.peruvianandes.com

Ayacucho and the central highlands
ACCOMMODATION
Marquez de Valdelirios ★
Ignore overpriced options and head here instead.
Alameda Bolognesi 720, Ayacucho.
Tel: (066) 818 944.
La Colmena ★★
A true oasis of calm. Ask for a room with a balcony overlooking the lush courtyard full of colourful birds.
Cusco 140, Ayacucho.
Tel: (066) 311 318.

EATING OUT
Tripico Upricha ★★
Come here for Peruvian cuisine at its best, not rushed, not over-intricate – just fresh ingredients lovingly prepared in a relaxed and beautiful atmosphere.
Jirón Londres 272, Ayacucho.
Tel: (066) 813 905.

CUSCO AND MACHU PICCHU
Cusco
ACCOMMODATION
Hostal Marani ★★
Dutch-run and full of character, this hotel with en-suite bathrooms is built round a courtyard in the artists' district and offers free transfers from the airport. It is closely associated with community projects.
Carmen Alto 194, San Blas.
Tel: (084) 249 462.
www.hostalmarani.com
Cusco Plaza ★★★
Part of a very reasonably priced Peruvian chain that has hotels in Cusco as well as in Lima, Nazca, Arequipa and Puno. Cosy and close to the Plaza de Armas, it has Wi-Fi and one room with disabled access.
Portal Espinar 142.
Tel: (084) 231 733.
www.casa-andina.com
Monasterio ★★★★
Historic, five-star hotel, and also one of the best in South America, in a 17th-century monastery in the heart of Cusco. An exquisite courtyard, good

restaurant and even its own chapel.
Calle Palacios 136, Plazoleta Nazarenas.
Tel: (084) 241 777.
www.monasterio.orient-express.com

EATING OUT
La Tertulia ★
Breakfast is particularly good here with a buffet of eggs, fruit, wholemeal bread and yoghurt. Linger over the free newspapers and stay for the bargain set lunch.
Procuradores 44, 2nd Floor. Tel: (084) 241 422.
Open: 6.30am–11pm.
Kusikuy ★★
The name of this restaurant, which serves up Andean and international cuisine, means 'Happy Guinea Pig' in Quechua. Try Peru's most celebrated dish, guinea pig baked in the oven.
Calle Plateros 348.
Tel: (084) 262 870.
Inca Grill ★★★
The international dishes, which include plenty of vegetarian choices, are good, but the main attraction is the nightly folkloric show.

Reservations essential.
Portal de Panes 115,
Plaza de Armas.
Tel: (084) 262 992.

Tunupa ★★★
A large menu specialising in Nouvelle Andean cuisine. Arrive from 6pm for a table on the balcony to see the sunset over the main square, and to avoid the tour groups.
Portal Confituria 233,
Plaza des Armas.
Tel: (084) 252 936.

ENTERTAINMENT

Cross Keys
One of Cusco's first pubs is very much a gringo affair, where tourists flock to watch football on cable TV, play darts and eat chicken curry. It's just as much a daytime haunt as a night-time boozer.
Confiturias 233,
Plaza de Armas.
Open: 11am–1am;
happy hour 6–7pm.

Mama Africa
International backpackers mix happily with locals at Cusco's best disco. This old favourite plays everything from techno to reggae, and shows videos in the afternoon to eager barflies.
Corner of Calle Triunfo and Santa Catalina. Free admission before 11pm with a pass handed out in Plaza de Armas.

Machu Picchu

ACCOMMODATION

Machu Picchu Pueblo Hotel ★★★★
Just 30 minutes by shuttle bus to Machu Picchu, pretty one- and two-storey cottages on the mountainside imitate an Andean village. A wonderful location with a lovely garden and cloud-forest walks, although the many steps are challenging at this altitude. It is justifiably part of the prestigious Small Luxury Hotels of the World group, with prices to match. Get a suite if you can.
Km 110 on the railway line, Aguas Calientes.
Tel: (084) 211 122.
www.inkaterra.com

Machu Picchu Sanctuary Lodge ★★★★
Just 200m (220yds) from the park entrance, this is the only hotel anywhere near Machu Picchu, allowing visitors to enjoy the magic of the area around the citadel away from the daytime hordes. There is an orchard garden and a full range of tours on offer. If you can afford it, don't miss a chance to stay here.
Machu Picchu.
Tel: (084) 242 3428.
www.sanctuarylodge.net

Rupa Wasi Condor House Eco Lodge ★★★★
Arguably the best hotel to stay in Aguas Calientes, Machu Picchu's nearest town. Spectacular views, beautiful exotic gardens, individually decorated colonial rooms and friendly service.
Calle Huanacaure 110,
Aguas Calientes.
Tel: (084) 211 001.
www.rupawasi.net

EATING OUT

Chez Maggy ★★
Whether you are after Peruvian food, pizza or even Mexican food, this is the place to go. You can't go wrong with a wood-fired pizza washed down with a Pisco Sour.

Avenida Pachacutec 156,
Aguas Calientes.
Tel: (084) 211 006.
Pueblo Viejo ★★
Live music makes this
one of the livelier places
in town. Local fare such
as trout, lamb and even
alpaca are on offer, but
there are vegetarian
dishes, too.
Avenida Pachacutec 108,
Aguas Calientes.
Tel: (084) 211 193.

The Sacred Valley
ACCOMMODATION
Sonesta Posada del
Inca ★★★★
An 18th-century convent
now houses this lovely
chain hotel with pretty
gardens. For those who
want to relax away from
the crowds.
Plaza Manco II de Yucay,
Urubamba 123. Tel: (084)
201 107.
www.sonesta.com

EATING OUT
Valle Sagrado ★★
Perhaps the best trout
you will find anywhere
in the area, plus great
lamb and plenty of
other choices.
Avenida Amazonas 116,
Pisac. Tel: (084) 203 009.

SPORT AND LEISURE
Eric Adventures
(Rafting)
One- and two-day
tours to the Urubamba
Valley running different
rapids according to level
of ability.
Calle Plateros 324, Cusco.
Tel: (084) 234 764.
www.ericadventures.com

AREQUIPA AND THE COLCA CANYON
ACCOMMODATION
Hostal Posada de
Sancho ★
Basic, but clean and
central with large rooms
and a roof terrace. The
staff can organise your
trip to the Colca Canyon.
Santa Catalina 213A,
Cercado, Arequipa.
Tel: (054) 287 797.
Email: posadasancho@
terra.com.pe
Hotel La Gruta ★★★
Close to the centre, 'The
Grotto' is a good place to
relax after an arduous
excursion to the Colca
Canyon. Try for a
garden room.
Calle La Gruta 304,
Selva Alegre, Arequipa.
Tel: (054) 224 631.
www.lagrutahotel.com

EATING OUT
Ary Quepay ★★
In all the guidebooks,
and justifiably so.
In the evening, live
music accompanies
traditional dishes.
Open for breakfast too.
Jerusalén 502, Arequipa.
Tel: (054) 672 922.
www.aryquepay.com
Tradición
Arequipeña ★★
Traditional food is not
the only big draw at this
restaurant: there is a
great view of El Misti –
if the weather is fine, ask
for a garden table. The
chupes (seafood soups)
are outstanding, as is
the *ceviche*. For the
best atmosphere,
visit when there is live
music.
Avenida Dolores 111,
Paucarpata, Arequipa.
Tel: (054) 242 385/
426 467.

ENTERTAINMENT
Déjà vu
Tasty lunches and
dinners, and a popular
drinking spot later. On
Friday night there is
live music, and on
Saturday a booming
Latin disco.

San Francisco 319,
Arequipa.
Tel: (054) 221 904.

SPORT AND LEISURE
Peru Adventure Tours
Mountain bikes, canyon
hikes and much more
from this accomplished
operator.
Jerusalén 410A, Arequipa.
Tel: (054) 221 658.
www.
peruadventuretours.com

LAKE TITICACA
ACCOMMODATION
All Ways Travel ★
This agency is highly
recommended and can
arrange homestays with
islanders on the lake as
well as accommodation
at the high-end ecolodge
on the island of Suasi.
Casa del Corregidor,
Calle Deustua 576, Puno.
Tel: (054) 355 552.
www.titicacaperu.com
Hostal Los Uros ★
This hotel is so cheap
that it is frequently full.
It's a great bargain,
but be prepared for
hot water appearing in
the evenings only.
Teodóro Valcárcel 135,
Puno. Tel: (054) 352 141.
www.losuros.com

Hotel Libertador Isla
Esteves ★★★
One of the more
comfortable options
in this area. Efficient and
friendly service.
Isla Esteves, Puno.
Tel: (054) 367 780.
www.libertador.com.pe

EATING OUT
Café Internacional ★
This is one of the better
restaurants in town,
with generous portions
of pasta and steak for
dinner and good
breakfast options too.
This is a place to come
for a good feed in simple
surroundings.
Corner of Libertad and
Moquegua, Puno.
Tel: (054) 352 502.
Restaurant Don
Piero ★★
Peruvian and
international fare is
on the menu at this
reliable restaurant that
welcomes tourists and
locals alike.
Jirón Lima 348–364, Puno
Tel: (054) 351 766.

SPORT AND LEISURE
Piramide Tours
A helpful and well-
organised agency,

offering trips to the
islands of Lake Titicaca,
as well as to Sillustani.
Jirón Deza 129, Puno.
Tel: (054) 367 302.
www.titikakalake.com

THE AMAZON
Iquitos and the
northern Amazon
ACCOMMODATION
All the jungle lodges
listed here are considered
to have good eco
credentials and are a fair
distance from Iquitos.
Prices are high because
meals, transport and
transfers (sometimes up
to four or five hours) are
included. If you choose
to stay at a lodge closer
to Iquitos, expect less
wildlife and a more
cavalier attitude to the
environment. In Iquitos
itself, accommodation is
cheap and plentiful
(www.andeantravelweb.
com).
Hostal Ambasador ★★
If you are not
transferring straight to
your jungle lodge, this
is a good option for a
day or two in the town
of Iquitos. Try to get
a room with air
conditioning.

Pevas 260, Iquitos.
Tel: (065) 231 618.
Fax: (065) 233 110.

Explorama ★★★
A large professional operator with five lodges in the jungle around Iquitos, and one of the few offering walks in the canopy (*see p106*).
Avenida La Marina 340, Iquitos.
Tel: (065) 252 530.
Fax: (065) 252 533.
www.explorama.com

Muyuna Amazon Lodge and Expeditions ★★★
Oil-burning lamps light the bungalows in this rustic but beautiful lodge.
Putumayo 163, 1st Floor, Iquitos.
Tel: (065) 242 858.
www.muyuna.com

Yacumama Lodge ★★★★
Safeguarding the environment was a priority when this lodge was built, so solar power and proper waste management, together with recycling and use of sustainable materials, were all high priorities. Choose from well-equipped rooms in the main

lodge or private bungalows – all thatch roofed and built by locals. You pay a premium, but meals are delicious and the lodge is so deep into the jungle that this is your best chance to see all the wildlife you could ever dream of.
Sargento Lores 149, Iquitos.
Tel: (065) 235 510.
www.
yacumamalodge.com

EATING OUT

Aris Burgers ★
A long-standing American diner in the jungle that always seems to be full of tourists tucking into the standard burgers and chips.
Próspero 127, Iquitos.
No telephone.

El Nuevo Mesón ★★
There are plenty of international dishes on offer here, but it is the exotic, regional specialities that stick in everyone's minds. How about fried lizard and chips?
Malecón Maldonado 153, Iquitos.
Tel: (065) 231 837.

Puerto Maldonado and the southern jungle
ACCOMMODATION

EcoAmazonia Lodge ★★★
Only 35km (22 miles) down the Madre de Dios River from Puerto Maldonado, this is a comfortable lodge, with good-value excursions.
Bookings: Calle Garcilaso 210, Office 206, Cusco.
Tel: (084) 236 159.
Fax: (084) 225 068.
www.ecoamazonia.com.pe

Pantiacolla Lodge ★★★
As a gateway to the unforgettable Manu Biosphere Reserve (*see p108*), this lodge has won praise for its all-encompassing approach, which includes Spanish lessons, birdwatching, night tours on the river and the chance to spot giant anteaters and otters.
Bookings: Calle Saphy 554, Cusco (main office).
Tel: (084) 238 323.
Fax: (084) 252 696.
www.pantiacolla.com

WASAI Tambopata Lodge & Research Center ★★★
Fifty kilometres (31 miles) from Puerto

Maldonado on the banks of the Tambopata River, this is a good place if you don't want a full-on jungle experience with constant trekking. The emphasis here is more on relaxation, although there are around 20km (12½ miles) of trails around the lodge if you're up to it.
Plaza Grau No 1,
Puerto Maldonado.
Tel/fax: (084) 572 290.
www.wasai.com

Heath River Wildlife Center ★★★★
Located on the edge of the pristine Bahuaja-Sonene, this is a five-hour river-boat journey from Puerto Maldonado. It is one of the best locations to try for ultra-rare sightings of jaguars and tapirs in the wild, not to mention the daily spectacle of 300 macaws getting their regular fix at the riverside clay lick.
Bookings: InkaNatura
Travel, Manuel Bañon
461, Lima 27.
Tel: (01) 440 2022.
www.inkanatura.com

THE NORTH COAST
Trujillo
ACCOMMODATION
Gran Bolívar Hotel ★★★
A charming hotel where the price includes transport from the airport. It seamlessly combines colonial style with modern amenities, but do not expect international standards of service.
Jirón Bolívar 957.
Tel: (044) 222 090.
www.perunorte.com/
granbolivar

Hotel Libertador ★★★
This luxury chain hotel on the main square is convenient for both Chán Chán and the airport. There is a good bar as well as a restaurant, pool and gym in which to relax after an archaeological tour.
Jirón Independencia 485,
Plaza de Armas.
Tel: (044) 232 741.
www.libertador.com.pe

Huanchaco
ACCOMMODATION
Las Palmeras ★★
A modern complex with a wide range of accommodation from single to family rooms. It is not far from the sea,

but there is a swimming pool in which to cool down after exploring the dusty historical sights in the region.
Avenida Larco No 1150,
Sector Los Tumbos.
Tel/fax: (044) 461 199.
www.
laspalmerasdehuanchaco.
com

EATING OUT
Otra Cosa ★
Should you tire of local seafood, or if you are a vegetarian who doesn't eat fish, pop into Otra Cosa (A Different Thing). Choose from the dish of the day, or the good-value set meal of a soup and a wholesome vegetable dish.
Avenida Victor Larco 921.
Tel: (044) 461 346.
www.otracosa.info.
Closed: After 8pm.

Club Colonial ★★
Enjoy an interesting mix of Belgian and Peruvian cuisine from crêpes to *ceviche* (raw fish marinated in lime juice) in an exquisite 18th-century mansion.
Grau 272.
Tel: (044) 461 015.
Closed: After 10pm.

Index

Acknowledgements

Thomas Cook Publishing wishes to thank IAIN MACINTYRE for the photographs in this book, to whom the copyright belongs, except for the following images:

DREAMSTIME.COM 1, 147 (Galyna Andrushko); 33 (Pavalache Stelian); 51 (Uros Ravbar)
FOTOLIA 139 (Yvonne Bogdanski)
PERUVIAN TOURIST BOARD 15, 47, 99, 105, 107
WIKIMEDIA COMMONS 17, 77
WORLD PICTURES/PHOTOSHOT 35

For CAMBRIDGE PUBLISHING MANAGEMENT LTD:
Project editor: Karen Beaulah
Copy editor: Joanne Osborn
Typesetter: Trevor Double
Proofreader: Ian Faulkner
Indexer: Karolin Thomas

SEND YOUR THOUGHTS TO
BOOKS@THOMASCOOK.COM

We're committed to providing the very best up-to-date information in our travel guides and constantly strive to make them as useful as they can be. You can help us to improve future editions by letting us have your feedback. If you've made a wonderful discovery on your travels that we don't already feature, if you'd like to inform us about recent changes to anything that we do include, or if you simply want to let us know your thoughts about this guidebook and how we can make it even better – we'd love to hear from you.

Send us ideas, discoveries and recommendations today and then look out for your valuable input in the next edition of this title.

Emails to the above address, or letters to Travellers Series Editor, Thomas Cook Publishing, PO Box 227, Coningsby Road, Peterborough PE3 8SB, UK.

Please don't forget to let us know which title your feedback refers to!